Robber and Hero

Joseph Lee Heywood, artist unknown
(Northfield Historical Society)

Robber and Hero
The Story of the Northfield Bank Raid

GEORGE HUNTINGTON

With an introduction by John McGuigan

MINNESOTA HISTORICAL SOCIETY PRESS
St. Paul • 1986

Borealis Books are high-quality paperback reprints of books chosen by the Minnesota Historical Society Press for their importance as enduring historical sources and their value as enjoyable accounts of life in the Upper Midwest.

MINNESOTA HISTORICAL SOCIETY PRESS, St. Paul, 55101

First published in 1895 by the Christian Way Co., Northfield, Minnesota
New material copyright © 1986 by the Minnesota Historical Society

International Standard Book Number 0-87351-194-8
Manufactured in the United States of America
10 9 8 7 6 5 4 3 2 1

Library of Congress Cataloging-in-Publication Data

Huntington, George, 1835–1916.
  Robber and Hero

  Reprint. Originally published: Northfield, Minn.: Christian Way Co., 1895.
  Includes index.
  1. Bank robberies—Minnesota—Northfield. I. Title.
HV6452.M62Y684 1986   364.1'552'0974413   86-16426
ISBN 0-87351-194-8

CONTENTS.

LIST OF ILLUSTRATIONS.

INTRODUCTION TO THE REPRINT EDITION.

In June of 1895, the southeastern Minnesota town of Northfield celebrated the twenty-fifth anniversary of the founding of one of its most prestigious institutions, Carleton College. While the local newspaper, *The Independent*, heralded the occasion on its front pages, a brief announcement was buried on page 5. "Robber and Hero," proclaimed the headline; the story described the publication of a new book, "an authentic history of the attempt to rob the First National Bank of this city, in 1876 . . . written in an entertaining and forcible manner, bringing the events that it portrays before the reader clearly, vividly and with historic exactness." The article outlined the book's contents chapter by chapter and gave the names of the town's defenders, including Joseph Lee Heywood, "the hero of the piece." Nowhere did it mention the names of the robbers.

Author's note: I would like to thank those residents of Northfield who helped me in my pursuit of fact and legend. Beverly Allers, director of the Northfield Historical Society, Marston Headley of the Northfield Public Library, attorney Lee Fossum, Marie Gery (a.k.a. "Zerelda Samuel"), *Northfield News* editor and columnist Maggie Lee, and Catherine and Bob Gjerdingen graciously lent time, information, and other assistance. Chip Demann, Jane Moline, committee chairman Greg Langer, and the mem-

On the same page, however, in an adjoining column of local notices, the public was informed, "Photographs of the Younger Brothers and one of their revolvers can be seen in Turner's window."[1]

The two notices referred, of course, to another, less public-spirited event that unfolded on the quiet Thursday afternoon of September 7, 1876, when a band of eight riders, wearing long linen "dusters" to conceal an armory of hand guns, raided the First National Bank of Northfield. That such a transgression should occur in a region that considered itself fully civilized by 1876 was unusual enough. Most of the town's citizens looked, and some traveled, eastward to the nation's centennial celebration in Philadelphia, while the news of Custer's demise two months earlier in Montana was evidence for the location of the real frontier. To an outsider, the Northfield of 1876 would seem in appearance and demeanor little different from any Yankee village of New England, the region most Northfielders once called home.[2]

bers of the planning committee for the 1985 Defeat of Jesse James Days opened their meetings and their homes. The members of the "James-Younger band"—Chuck, Chip, Doug, and Chris Demann, Wayne Eddy, Michael ("Doenuts") Douglas, Richard Eisinger, John Perkins, Dave Vickmark, and artist Derk Hansen (whose drawing adorns the cover of this edition)—helped turn the often tedious task of research into just plain fun.

[1] *The Independent* (Northfield), June 13, 1895, p.1.

[2] Kirk Jeffrey, "Bread and Butter," and Clifford Clark, "The Town as Manifested," in *Continuum: Threads in the Community Fabric of Northfield, Minnesota*, ed. Lynn Carlin (Northfield: Minnesota Bicentennial Commission, 1976), 40–61, 62–77. See also Lillie Clara Berg, *Early Pi-*

But it was not just Northfield's admirable attributes that made the event remarkable. This was the first attempted raid on a national bank, and the perpetrators were none other than Missouri's famous James-Younger gang: Jesse and Frank James; Thomas Coleman (Cole), James, and Robert Younger; William Stiles; William McClelland (Clel) Miller; and Charles Pitts. Already ten years into a career of robbery and murder, the James-Younger gang had achieved national notoriety through the auspices of newspaper editors who were eager to capitalize on smoldering sentiments for the "lost cause" of the Confederacy. The James and Younger brothers, taught by guerilla leaders William ("Bloody Bill") Anderson and William Clarke Quantrill, had served that cause; they learned their trade well enough to ensure their place in American frontier history as expert train robbers and peacetime originators of the daylight bank heist.[3]

---

oneers and Indians of Minnesota and Rice County (San Leandro, Calif.: Lillie Clara Berg, 1959), and L. E. Swanberg, ed., *Then and Now: A History of Rice County, Faribault, and Communities* (Faribault: Rice County Bi-Centennial Commission, 1976).

[3] For biographical information on the gang, here and below, see William A. Settle, Jr., *Jesse James Was His Name* (Columbia: University of Missouri Press, 1966; Lincoln: University of Nebraska Press, Bison Books, 1977). Settle's book remains the only scholarly history of Jesse James and his compatriots. In contrast to the scores of popular histories written about the James and Younger brothers, Settle's account is distinguished by its meticulous research, careful examination of sources, and balanced judgement. It is indispensible for sorting fact from myth. A fine summary of the raid itself is Walter Trenerry's "Highwaymen Came Riding," in *Murder in Minnesota* (St. Paul: Minnesota Historical Society, 1962; repr. ed., 1985).

The James-Younger brothers, in particular Jesse and Frank James and Cole Younger, had also become expert in the art of self-promotion. They astutely realized the potential of the mass media of the day, when news could travel almost instantaneously across a country linked by telegraph wire. In 1872 a newspaper editor in Missouri could write of these men: "It was as though three bandits had come to us from the storied Odenwald, with the halo of medieval chivalry upon their garments and shown us how things were done that poets sing of."[4] The occasion? A daylight robbery of the gate cashier at the Kansas City state fair, during which a girl was severely wounded by gunfire. In 1875 the bandits' image had been enhanced by the miscalculations of the Pinkerton National Detective Agency, whose detectives managed to maim Zerelda Samuel, mother of Jesse and Frank, and kill their nine-year-old half brother during a raid on the James residence outside Kearney, Missouri. When coupled with the well-publicized story of Jesse's marriage a year earlier, the assault on the James's matriarch added a potent dash of family virtue to the public image that circulated throughout the United States.

When George Huntington wrote *Robber and Hero*, almost two decades had passed since the raid on Northfield's bank; Cole and Jim Younger were serving life sentences in the Minnesota state prison at Stillwater (Robert had died of tuberculosis in the prison hospital in 1889); Jesse James

---

[4] *Kansas City Times*, Sept. 27, 1872, quoted in Settle, *Jesse James*, 46.

had lain in the grave for thirteen years; and Jesse's brother, Frank, was living a respectable life in Missouri as a starter for horse races, having been acquitted by sympathetic juries of all charges brought against him following his surrender to Missouri's governor, Thomas T. Crittenden, in 1882. Huntington, a professor of logic and rhetoric at Carleton College, had arrived at Northfield in 1879, just three years after the raid, having served for sixteen years as a Congregational minister in Rhode Island, Illinois, and his home state of Connecticut. True to Huntington's ministerial training, his literary output consisted mainly of "instructional" fiction and verse, hymns, and Biblical commentary. He was much concerned with the moral and religious education of youth and was active in Sunday school activities, the YMCA, and local improvement societies. As college professor, Huntington earned a reputation for leniency concerning student infractions, and though he was a less than efficient administrator, his character, kindness, and exuberant eccentricities were fondly appreciated by both colleagues and students.[5]

Huntington's Congregational affiliations were shared by Carleton College and by its former treasurer in 1876, Joseph Lee Heywood, the "hero" of this book who, as book-

---

[5] *Northfield News*, Jan. 7, 1916, p.1, 4; Leal A. Headley and Merrill E. Jarchow, *Carleton: The First Century* (Northfield: Carleton College, 1966), 138, 148, 182, 229, 243; Warren Upham, *Congregational Work of Minnesota, 1832–1920* (Minneapolis: Congregational Conference of Minnesota, 1921), 89, 170, 351, 494–97. Huntington also had a penchant for composing parodic verse and limericks. Huntington Papers, Minnesota Historical Society (hereafter MHS).

keeper and acting cashier of the First National Bank of Northfield, was shot dead by the would-be robbers. (The finger of suspicion still points to either Jesse or Frank James as the actual triggerman.) Under different circumstances, Joseph Heywood would doubtless have lived out his life with quiet distinction, just the sort of community pillar who, throughout the history of American frontier expansion, symbolized the ultimate and inevitable progress of civil conduct and civilized standards. When confronted by three armed men demanding entrance to the bank's vault, the quiet bookkeeper refused to open the safe contained within the vault (a safe that, unbeknownst to the robbers, was actually unlocked), and thus assumed for the people of Northfield the mantle of martyr and hero.

The making of a hero can be a relatively simple matter. To a community removed by just a couple of decades from early settlement and only one decade from bloody civil war and Indian uprising, heroism was synonymous with selflessly risking or forfeiting one's life in the service of some higher cause. Heroic legend, however, can be another matter altogether, and often depends not so much on actual events as it does on subsequent *perceptions* of events and of the people or person associated with those events. In 1936 the British folklorist Lord Raglan developed a list, or typology, of characteristics common to European legendary heroes.[6] Other scholars built on Raglan's fundamental premise, which suggested that even in the absence of veri-

---

[6] Lord Raglan (Fitz Roy Richard Somerset Raglan), *The Hero: A Study in Tradition, Myth, and Drama* (London: Metuen, 1936). See also Jan de Vries, *Heroic Song and Heroic Legend*, trans. B. J. Trimmer (London: Ox-

fiable data the life and actions of a "hero" would still be recounted according to certain commonly accepted criteria,
or rules, that defined the concept of "hero." In short, heroes
are made, not born. For an America attuned to Puritan
jeremiad, violent frontier confrontation, populist tradi-
tions, and sectional rivalries, fine points of law made little
impact on the public's choice of hero figures. Someone who
was legally an outlaw could just as well symbolize the felt
injustices of a region or a class of people with which the
outlaw was identified – hardly an outlandish notion when
one considers the endurance of the Robin Hood legend on
both sides of the Atlantic Ocean. And like Raglan's ancient
heroes, the outlaw-heroes of the American frontier were in-
vested with a common set of attributes that formed the
framework on which the details of their lives – real and
invented – were hung. Hence, hardened killers like Jesse
James, John Wesley Hardin, and Billy the Kid were transformed into pious, kind-hearted, daring, clever, even im-
mortal, hero figures for large, usually regional, segments of
the American population.[7]

ford University Press, 1963; New York: Arno Press, 1978), and Eric J.
Hobsbawn, *Primitive Rebels* (Manchester: Manchester University Press,
1959).

[7] On the outlaw-hero of the American West, see Richard E. Meyer,
"The Outlaw: A Distinctive American Folktype," *Journal of the Folklore
Institute* 17 (1980): 94–124, and Kent Ladd Steckmesser, *The Western
Hero in History and Legend* (Norman: University of Oklahoma Press,
1965). By far the best and most comprehensive analysis of the outlaw-hero
legend is Stephen Tatum's *Inventing Billy the Kid: Visions of the Outlaw
in America, 1881–1981* (Albuquerque: University of New Mexico Press,
1982).

Immediately following the Northfield raid, the town's citizens and the American banking community hailed Joseph Lee Heywood as their own hero. In his funeral address, the Reverend D.L. Leonard described Heywood as a man "modest and timid . . . conscientious through and through," who "in the sight of thousands . . . has been translated without seeing death, and was caught up from the earth to heaven as in a chariot of fire." Of Heywood's killers, he charged, "How quick will their memory rot, but how long will the memory of their victim be green and fragrant!"[8] Although banks throughout the United States would contribute over $17,000 to a memorial fund for Heywood's widow and daughter (see pages 101-19), Northfield's citizens soon realized the unintended irony of Leonard's predictions concerning the persistence of memory.

Within twenty-four hours after the Northfield raid, newspapers across the country carried the news of its presumed perpetrators, the James-Younger gang. In Minnesota, the shoot-out in Northfield was merely a prelude to the chase that followed. Although two members of the gang lay dead on Northfield's Division Street, slain by the alert hardware merchant, Anselm Manning, and medical student Henry Wheeler, the remaining six raiders fled to the southwest, short of horses and, in the case of Cole and Bob Younger, carrying lead souvenirs furnished by Manning

[8] D. L. Leonard, *Funeral Discourse of Joseph Lee Heywood* (Minneapolis: Johnson and Smith, 1876), 15.

and Wheeler. That a manhunt was even possible was due largely to the death in Northfield of gang member Bill Stiles, a Minnesota native who was the gang's guide and probably the instigator of the Minnesota expedition. As Huntington notes (page 51), five hundred men, with more following, were on the trail within two days. Policemen from Minneapolis and St. Paul were joined by Civil War General John Pope and a complementary army of newspaper reporters who daily recounted the news "from the Front" for their readers.[9] Two weeks later, after the trail had gone cold, four of the outlaws – the three Younger brothers and Charles Pitts – were discovered and cornered in Hanska Slough near Madelia, Minnesota. After a fierce exchange of gunfire, only Bob Younger could stand and surrender; Pitts was dead, while Cole and Jim Younger were wounded several times. Although both Frank and Jesse James had earlier separated from the Younger contingent and escaped the cordon, the capture of the Youngers was sufficient cause for celebration. Local photographers Ira E. Sumner, Elias F. Everett, and William H. Jacoby, capitalizing on the public mood, sold nearly fifty thousand souvenir sets of photographs portraying the quite dead

[9] See, for example *St. Paul Dispatch*, Sept. 11, 1876, p.1 ("Very Latest from Front"); *St. Paul and Minneapolis Pioneer Press and Tribune*, Sept. 10, 1876, p. 1 ("The Seat of War"); and Sept. 14, 1876, p. 1 ("The Commissary Department of the Enemy . . . at a Fearfully Low Ebb"). The rhetoric of war has also been extended to metaphorical comparisons, most commonly in reference to the Northfield raid as either "the Gettysburg" or "the Waterloo" of the James-Younger gang.

raiders.[10] A month later, "Our Missouri Bandits," as they were termed by one newspaper, were installed for life in the state prison in Stillwater, after pleading guilty to avoid trial and possible execution.[11]

Against this backdrop of hyperbole and confusion, the memory of Northfield's dead "hero" quickly receded. If anything, the defeat of the James-Younger gang only magnified its reputation, adding fuel to the legendary process already well established before 1876.[12] In Minnesota, certainly, the enhancement of the gang's reputation was necessary to justify the attention accorded the chase and capture – not to mention the praise awarded to the participants of the chase and, by extension, the entire state. After all, if one defeats a hero in honorable contest, one can thereby become a hero. The key word here is "honorable"; that lesson was borne out six years later when Jesse James was shot from behind while dusting a picture in the parlor of his house in St. Joseph, Missouri. His killer was a fellow gang member, the "dirty little coward" Robert Ford, who

---

[10] The photographs by Sumner, Everett, and Jacoby continue to be sold at the shop in the restored First National Bank museum in Northfield. Curiously, or perhaps naturally, none of their obituaries mentions the Northfield raid photographs: *Minneapolis Journal*, May 22, 1880, p. 4; *Northfield News*, Sept. 17, 1904, p. 11; *Northfield Independent*, July 11, 1918, p. 1. For information and citations about the photographers, I am indebted to John Dougherty, MHS.

[11]*St. Paul and Minneapolis Pioneer Press and Tribune*, Nov. 19, 1876, p. 2.

[12] On the role of defeat in heroic legend, see Bruce A. Rosenberg, *Custer and the Epic of Defeat* (University Park: Pennsylvania State University Press, 1974).

had arranged a deal with Missouri Governor Crittenden for an alleged reward. Jesse's death at the hands of a traitor, followed by well-reported scenes of his grieving widow and children, became the final, indispensable element in the hero-making process.

That process had gained momentum in the early 1880s with the publication of dime novels purporting to relate the sensational and fantastic exploits of the James brothers.[13] By 1895, as George Huntington notes in his preface, the facts of the raid were hardly known "to a generation of young people now growing up" (page xlii). (One need look no further than to the newspaper notices quoted at the start of this introduction for a graphic demonstration of Huntington's lament. The mere mention of the Younger brothers was sufficient advertisement for the display in Turner's window, whereas the ad for *Robber and Hero* required a lengthy description of its contents – in effect, of the raid itself.) Furthermore, Missouri sympathizers had attempted since 1885 to secure pardons for the imprisoned Younger brothers, and within ten years, considerable support for pardon had been generated even in Minnesota.[14]

---

[13] See, for example, W. D. Stevens [John R. Musick], *The James Boys in Minnesota* (New York: Wide Awake Library, 1882), and Horst H. Kruse, "Myth in the Making: The James Brothers, the Bank Robbery at Northfield, Minn., and the Dime Novel," *Journal of Popular Culture* 10 (Fall 1976): 315–24.

[14] For a complete, if biased, history of the campaign to pardon the Youngers, see Warren Carter Bronaugh, *The Youngers' Fight for Freedom* (Columbia, Mo.: E. W. Stephens Publishing Co., 1906). Bronaugh, a Missouri infantry officer in the Confederate army, led the effort to free the Youngers from Stillwater prison.

By the mid-1890s, the American West had been, for the most part, tamed and settled, and the wounds of Civil War and Reconstruction were largely healed if not forgotten. Likewise, the exploits of the Old West's most celebrated characters, lawmen and outlaws alike, had become the stuff of nostalgia. Popular ballads could recount the story of a Jesse James who was "a friend to the poor" and who "could never see a man suffer pain," or of that "reckless highwayman," Cole Younger.[15] (Even so cold-blooded a killer as John Wesley Hardin would be pardoned in 1894 by the governor of Texas.) By behaving as model prisoners, the Youngers, especially the consummate actor, Cole, had managed to gain the sympathy of their captors, and the wasting death of handsome Bob Younger in 1889 only served to magnify the "plight" of the Stillwater prison's famous residents.

As might be expected, many citizens of Northfield were less than happy about the continuing efforts to pardon the Youngers. But the town's protests, though sometimes acknowledged, were hardly sufficient to offset the roster of pardon supporters that read like a *Who's Who* of early Minnesota: former governors Henry H. Sibley, Alexander

[15] See, for example, Norm Cohen, *Long Steel Rail: The Railroad in American Folksong* (Urbana: University of Illinois Press, 1981), 97–121; John A. Lomax, *Cowboy Songs and Other Frontier Ballads* (New York: Macmillan, 1910), 27–28, 106–7; and John A. Lomax and Alan Lomax, *American Ballads and Folk Songs* (New York: Macmillan, 1934), 128–31. The ballad "Cole Younger" includes lines about the Northfield raid: "The robbing of the Northfield Bank, the same I can't deny,/For now I am a prisoner, in Stillwater jail I lie" (Lomax, *Cowboy Songs*, 106).

Ramsey, and William R. Marshall; Senators Cushman K. Davis and Dwight Sabin; author and politician Ignatius Donnelly; Bishop Henry Whipple; Stillwater prison warden Henry Wolfer; three members of the posse that captured the Youngers; and many others. From Missouri came petitions signed by successive governors and legislatures; Thomas Crittenden, the same man who, as governor, had "broken" the James gang, wrote to the Minnesota Board of Pardons in 1897 to "beg" for the Youngers' pardon.[16]

Northfield responded with strongly worded petitions and letters protesting the pardon of Cole and Jim Younger. In addition to the sympathies he clearly expressed in *Robber and Hero*, George Huntington noted in a newspaper interview supplementing news of a Northfield petition:

> I was not in Northfield at the time of the raid and have never seen the robbers. I have no vindictive feeling against them. Their punishment, longer or shorter, is no gratification to me. I am sincerely sorry for them and respect the kindheartedness of those who are seeking to procure their release. But it is by neither vengeful nor compassionate feeling that the question of pardon should be determined. That question is just as judicial as the question of their original guilt. . . . I am pleased to know that a certain prisoner [Cole Younger] has been well behaved in prison. His good conduct was not only commendable, but greatly to his own advantage, and he has had the benefit of it in the mitigation

[16] Bronaugh, *Youngers' Fight*, 95, 97, 105–9, 120–22, 127–28, 179–80.

of his lot as a convict. But if every well behaved
convict is to be released, we shall have a wholesale
jail delivery. The purpose of confining these robbers is not to inflict suffering upon them, but to
deter other men from similar crimes; to increase
the safety of property and life; to make it possible
for men like Mr. Heywood to perform their
honest duties without risk of assassination.[17]

Given the climate of popular opinion, Huntington's
choice of title, *Robber and Hero*, was an appropriate, if inadequate, reminder of just who should be celebrated. Based
on interviews with the participants and on other primary
source materials, the book remains the most authoritative
account of the raid. However, it seems to have had little impact on Huntington's contemporaries, at least those in
whose power was held the fate of the imprisoned outlaws.[18]

The only obstacle preventing pardon as early as 1897 was
Cole Younger's refusal to name the man who pulled the
trigger on Joseph Heywood. Younger had declined to pro-
vide the name since his capture, when he scribbled a note
in response to his captors' questions: "Be true to your
friends/If the heavens fall."[19] When interviewed in 1897,
Frank James contributed to the image of noble sufferance

[17] *St. Paul Daily Pioneer Press*, July 6, 1897, p. 3. See also Bronaugh,
Youngers' Fight, 198–99.

[18] None of the obituaries of George Huntington mention *Robber and
Hero* among his published works. See *Northfield News*, Jan. 7, 1916, p. 1;
E. M. Williams, "Rev. Geo. Huntington," *Congregational Minnesota* 9
(Feb. 1916), 2.

[19] Collections of the Northfield Historical Society.

by noting (no doubt with some relief): "The Younger boys
refused to accept liberty, accompanied by the dishonor of
placing the responsibility for a part in the Northfield crime
upon some former comrade. There is an unwritten law
among men like the Youngers that makes them honorable
to each other unto death."[20] Although temporarily frus-
trated, the Youngers had, in effect, made a deposit in the
bank of popular opinion that they drew on four years later,
when the Minnesota legislature passed the Deming Bill,
which for the first time allowed the parole of prisoners serving life sentences. The bill's sponsor, Portius C. Deming,
did not disguise his intent to aid in the release of Cole and
Jim Younger, and his name on the legislation was soon re-
placed by that of "Younger" in unofficial circles. On July
14, 1901, one month after the bill's passage, the Youngers
walked through the gates of Stillwater Prison and into a
world much changed since 1876. The terms of their parole
forbade their leaving Minnesota, and their employment as
tombstone salesmen had been arranged before their release
by Warden Wolfer and the state parole board.[21]

It is hardly surprising that some people, after lengthy imprisonment, find it difficult to adjust to life on the "outside." As parolees, Cole and Jim Younger were restricted
in their movements and choices of employment. Although

[20]*St. Paul Daily Pioneer Press*, July 15, 1897, p. 4.

[21] Bronaugh, *Youngers' Fight*, 229–35. See also Younger Brothers Inmate Case Files, Stillwater State Prison, in Northfield (Minnesota) Bank
Robbery of 1876 Collections and Stillwater State Prison Case Files,
microfilm edition, MHS.

no longer confined behind prison walls, the brothers remained, for all intents and purposes, wards of the state, prohibited from passing beyond its borders. Always the extrovert and opportunist, Cole Younger seemed at ease with his new circumstances. Brother Jim, however, was nearly opposite in temperament. Diffident and moody as a prisoner, he had always relied on his older brother for guidance and support. A disfiguring facial wound, sustained in the shoot-out at Madelia twenty-five years earlier, had left him with a severe speech impediment, an inability to eat solid foods, and a bullet lodged in his upper jaw near the base of the brain. In the parole reports regularly filed by the brothers, Cole's sanguinity contrasts sharply with Jim's increasing despondency.[22]

Although he was unable to hold down a permanent job and short of money, Jim's spirits were bouyed for a short while by a romance with a St. Paul reporter, Alix Mueller, who had befriended him while he was still a prisoner. Five months after his release, however, Jim's world came crashing down around him. The parole board denied him permission to marry Alix on the grounds that as a parolee he was still a life prisoner and therefore legally unable to bind himself to any contract, even a marriage contract. Despite pleas to a sympathetic governor, no legal loopholes were found, and a despondent Alix left Minnesota to escape the publicity that had surrounded her romance. By the fall of 1902, Jim's situation was desperate. Out of touch with

[22] Younger Brothers Inmate Case Files.

Cole, who was by then employed by St. Paul police chief John O'Connor, Jim had long been out of work, unable to apply what he called "the signature of a dead man" to offered contracts of employment. On October 13, Jim's request for a full pardon had been denied, and within a few days he was talking of suicide as the only logical alternative left to a man who was "only a ghost."[23] In the early morning of October 19, Jim Younger, alone in his hotel lodging, fired a bullet into his brain. In a suicide note, written to his "Lassie," Jim proclaimed himself a Socialist, "decidedly in favor of woman's rights," and he condemned politicians and the pardon board who failed to pity "the man that knows how to love, and appreciate a friend in truth."[24] Four days later he was buried near his home in Lee's Summit, Missouri, next to the grave of his brother-in-arms, Bob. As might be expected, Jim Younger's pathetic end was cause for journalistic reminders of "the long arm of retribution" that awaits "the trespasser against human and divine law."[25]

Jim's suicide also proved to be helpful to Cole when, four months later, he was granted a full pardon by what was probably a contrite board of pardons. The pardon was not without conditions, however. Prevented from leaving Minnesota while under parole, Cole was now enjoined from ever returning to the state. Furthermore, Cole had to promise that he would never exhibit himself for public amuse-

[23] *Minneapolis Tribune*, Oct. 21, 1902, p. 7.

[24] *Minneapolis Tribune*, Oct. 20, 1902, p. 1.

[25] *Minneapolis Tribune*, Oct. 21, 1902, p. 4.

ment where admission fees might be charged. Cole interpreted this injunction liberally, for soon after his return to Missouri, he teamed up with his old confederate, Frank James, to become part owner of the "Cole Younger and Frank James' Historical Wild West Show." Although he professed never to take part in any show activities, and regularly delivered a moral lecture on "What My Life Has Taught Me," Cole's use of his own name and his regular appearance in the show's celebrity box was considered by many a breach of his promise to the board of pardons.[26] In 1904 Cole petitioned the state of Minnesota for an unconditional pardon with the hope of bringing the show – a second-rate carnival at best – to what he surmised to be lucrative territory. Cole's former friend and supporter, warden Henry Wolfer, responded frankly:

> You have not only violated the spirit of your pardon but you have, by your conduct, outraged every principle of manhood. Among your old Missouri friends you had the reputation of being a brave man, but your treatment of Minnesota and your old friends in this State convinces me that you are a coward.[27]

Soon thereafter the show folded, and Frank James retired with his wife to the family farm until his death in 1915; Cole remained on the lecture circuit for several years until

[26] Thomas Coleman Younger, *The Story of Cole Younger, By Himself* (Chicago: Henneberry Co., 1903), 104–23.

[27] Henry Wolfer to Cole Younger, Feb. 9, 1905, Younger Brothers Inmate Case Files.

death finally stilled the old trouper in 1916. He never returned to Minnesota.

Long before the deaths of Cole and Frank, Jesse James had been enshrined in the pantheon of American popular heroes, and the exploits of Jesse, Frank, and Cole had become raw material for virtually all forms of popular entertainment, from dime novels to stage plays. If anything, Frank and Cole remained until their deaths prisoners of Jesse's image. By the early twentieth century, the legend of Jesse James had outpaced any attempts to confine it within the limits of documented fact. Like the merging of the medieval Robin Hood with later figures such as Maid Marian and Friar Tuck, stories of the James-Younger gang were joined to those of other western outlaws, ranging from Billy the Kid to the notorious Belle Starr, who in one newspaper report was identified as a member of the gang that raided Northfield![28] Newspapers in St. Paul, Minneapolis, and large cities throughout the country never failed to print a good story, true or untrue, so long as it sold papers.

The advent of motion pictures created yet another venue for Jesse James, who was the subject of at least eight silent movies produced by 1927.[29] Typically, the movies had little to do with fact, pandering instead to popular expectations of a wild west show. In Minnesota, as elsewhere, protection under the First Amendment had not yet been extended to the new medium; officials in St. Paul, Min-

[28] *St. Paul Globe*, Feb. 13, 1903, p. 1.
[29] I am indebted to John Dougherty of the MHS for compiling and documenting information on movies and stage productions.

neapolis, and Faribault (county seat of Rice County, home also of Northfield) felt no constraints in 1911 to banning and seizing films about Jesse James, ostensibly to protect the morals of the impressionable youth who flocked to the movie houses.[30] Despite such gestures, in the subsequent seventy-four years no fewer than thirty-seven Jesse James "talkies" were filmed for theater and television, perhaps a record for any one subject. On the silver screen, the First National Bank of Northfield has been raided time and again by Henry Fonda, Tyrone Power, Robert Wagner, Cliff Robertson, Robert Duvall, David Carradine, Stacy Keach, and a host of others. Residents of Northfield have watched their town portrayed by sets located from Georgia to Oregon, complete with Cascade Mountains backdrop.[31] The recording industry has also capitalized on Jesse James, issuing more than 150 commercial recordings of ballads, traditional and newly composed, by the 1980s.[32]

George Huntington's sense of subdued, slightly pious dismay over the national fascination with Jesse James be-

---

[30] *St. Paul Daily News*, Oct. 5, 1911, p. 3; *St. Paul Pioneer Press*, Oct. 5, 1911, p. 3; Oct. 9, 1911, p. 3; Oct. 14, 1911, p. 14; *Faribault Journal*, Oct. 11, 1911, p. 1.

[31] For examples of local reactions, see *Northfield News*, Jan. 19, 1939, p. 1 ("Northfield Outraged by Jesse James Film Story"); Jan. 26, 1939, p. 1; Feb. 2, 1939, p. 1; May 18, 1972, p. 1; *St. Paul Pioneer Press*, May 2, 1977, p. 7 ("Raid Movie Is Insult to Northfield"). See also Don Graham, "*The Great Northfield Minnesota Raid* and the Cinematic Legend of Jesse James," *Journal of Popular Film* 6 (1977): 77–85, reprinted in Laura Butler, ed., *Western Movies* (Albuquerque: University of New Mexico Press, 1979), 131–37.

[32] For a complete discography, see Cohen, *Long Steel Rail*, 113–16, 121.

came a recurrent characteristic of Northfield's attitude toward the raid. Justifiably proud of its educational institutions (St. Olaf College had opened there in 1875) and agricultural prosperity, the town of "Cows, Colleges, and Contentment" maintained an aloof posture that remained unshaken even upon the fiftieth anniversary of the raid, when "officials of the First National Bank . . . frowned on any plan to dramatize the event because of its effect on the youth of a day when bank robberies are not so infrequent." In recounting the events of a half century earlier, local newspapers focused on the "lesson" of ordinary people who rose to an extraordinary challenge, a lesson relevant in 1926 "when indifference, selfishness, and a lack of common interest prodominate in most of the relationships of life."[33] The strength of this sentiment was demonstrated six years later, when the Minnesota Historical Society was forced to withdraw its proposal for a historical marker commemorating the raid. Northfield's citizens objected strenuously, arguing that the city's "social and educational history should first be commemorated" and that the marker's inscription failed to emphasize "the really heroic lesson" of the event.[34]

Apart from an occasional newspaper comment upon the deaths of townspeople who defended the First National Bank in 1876 and responses to Hollywood's various historical transgressions, Northfiield's pose of indifference re-

[33] *Northfield News*, Sept. 10, 1926, p. 2, 3. See also *Northfield News,* Jan. 1, 1926, p. 4; Aug. 27, 1926, p. 4; Sept. 3, 1926, p. 1, 9; Sept. 17, 1926, p. 4; and *St. Paul Pioneer Press*, Sept. 5, 1926, p. 4.
[34] *Northfield News*, Sept. 23, 1932, p. 4.

mained largely unbroken until 1947. That year the newly formed Northfield Jaycees announced plans to stage in 1948 the first local re-enactment of the raid as part of the town's annual Fall Festival. By this time, most of the town's citizens were at least a generation removed from the events of 1876, and World War II had bred a cadre of young veterans eager "to be where the action was."[35] Although the re-enactment of "Jesse James Days" seemed little different from the oft-criticized movies of the time, its success in generating publicity, crowds, and, of course, money, guaranteed its survival in subsequent years.

The re-enactment also highlighted divisions within the town that had not been so apparent in prior years. For example, the announcement in 1948 of the appearance of the last claimant to Jesse James's identity created a small storm that resulted in the withdrawal of the invitation, and one letter to the editor went so far as to suggest that Northfield invite Adolf Hitler to celebrate "Hitler Day" ("I understand some people think he is alive too," the correspondent noted).[36] Attempts were made in subsequent years to mollify public opinion by changing the name of the festival to "Defeat of Jesse James Days" but few were fooled by the change – the new banners displayed the words "Defeat of"

[35] Charles E. Demann, interview, Dundas, Minn., July 20, 1985. See also the following 1948 issues of *JC*, the newsletter of the Northfield Junior Chamber of Commerce: Apr. 27; June 1, 22, 26; July 6, 13; Aug. 3, 10, 17, 24, 31; Sept. 7, 14, 21.

[36] *Northfield News*, July 8, 1948, p. 1; July 15, 1948, p. 3; Aug. 12, 1948, p. 2 (quotation); Sept. 16, 1948, p. 3. See also *JC*, July 6 and 13, 1948.

in small letters above the large legend, "Jesse James Days." By the centennial year of 1976 (or bicentennial, depending on one's preference for markers) the festival had been transformed by a new generation of participants into something more closely resembling a historically accurate re-enactment, with the recently restored First National Bank of 1876 as backdrop. In the 1980s the Defeat of Jesse James Days each September drew more than fifty thousand people who enjoyed a host of sanctioned events, including tractor pulls, bicycle races, queen coronation, rodeo, carnivals, parade, celebrity grand marshals – and, of course, several re-enactments of the raid itself.

As the festival grew in size, attracting larger audiences from around the world, the debate over its propriety, which one wag called "Northfield's case of schizophrenia," became as much a part of Northfield's identity as its colleges. From mock burials of the "ghost" of Jesse James to the appearance of Jesse James's grandson in the festival parade in 1976, it would seem by all appearances that Jesse had finally conquered in death the town that thwarted him while he was alive.[37] Or, as locals prefer to put it, has Northfield captured Jesse? A comparison of Jesse's profits with those of the town itself following each festival weekend makes a strong case for the latter claim.

Citizens of Northfield and elsewhere often ask, "What's the *meaning* of Jesse James?" There is no simple answer, for

[37] *Northfield News*, Sept. 10, 1981, p. 2; Sept. 7, 1961, p. 1, 2; Sept. 16, 1976, p. 1, 12.

each generation creates its own meaning, depending on shifts of social and cultural mood and historical circumstances. But perhaps one constant runs throughout the maze of interpretations of Jesse James and other outlaw heroes. Stephen Tatum, in his perceptive and thorough analysis of the legends surrounding that other famous outlaw hero of the American West, Billy the Kid, notes a "dialectic of success and failure as related to the apparently basic human need for an intensely exciting, unpredictable world and for an ordered, secure, routine world." While the outlaw may fulfill "the old childhood dreams of belonging to a band of brothers, to a community of sympathetic spirits," he " must ultimately die in order for the community to exist in the present and to anticipate the future. . . . If the outlaw hero is successful only as a defeated delivering hero in legend, not as a successful hero in history, there is ultimately safety in his defeat, for this subversive figure's challenge to our perhaps too easy acceptance of life as it is becomes removed safely into the legendary past."[38] This explanation seems to carry with it more than a germ of truth and fits neatly into the scheme of Northfield's own, legendary conflict of attitudes about its famous visitors in 1876.

To the people of Northfield, however, the "meaning" of Jesse James also involves a justifiable pride in uncommon local accomplishment. Nowhere is this more evident than at the local elementary school, where hundreds of children

[38] Tatum, *Inventing Billy the Kid*, 195, 196, 197.

are gathered before each year's festival to hear of their town's heroism, as related by the costumed men who re-enact the raid on Northfield's streets. At the end of each program, in answer to the question, "Who is the hero of the Northfield Raid?" the children shout, "Northfield!" They never forget it.

— *JOHN McGUIGAN*

A NOTE ABOUT THE TEXT.

Robber and Hero, originally published in 1895, has seen at least two subsequent printings: one issued in pamphlet form in 1960 by the College City Press of Northfield, and a clothbound edition, with an informative introduction by Stan Nelson, published in 1962 by Ross and Haines of Minneapolis. Other publications devoted solely to the raid include:

John Jay Lemon [pseudonym of Joseph Have Hanson]. *The Northfield Tragedy; or The Robber's Raid*. Minneapolis: John Jay Lemon, 1876. A rare account drawn almost exclusively from St. Paul and Minneapolis newspapers. Huntington credits Lemon on p. xliii.

Dallas Cantrell, *Youngers' Fatal Blunder: Northfield, Minnesota*. San Antonio: Naylor Co., 1973. An extensive account, though inadequately documented and sophomoric in tone. (The author was nineteen when she wrote the book.)

The Northfield Bank Raid (Northfield: Northfield News, 1926). A twenty-two page compilation of stories published in the *Northfield News* upon the fiftieth anniversary of the raid.

The Northfield Raid (Northfield: Northfield News, 1933).
A thirty-two page pamphlet drawn from *Robber and Hero*
and from the 1926 *Northfield News* articles reprinted in the
preceding publication.

For a thorough listing and analysis of books about the
James-Younger brothers, see Ramon F. Adams's annotated
bibliographies, *Six-Guns and Saddle Leather* (Norman:
University of Oklahoma Press, 1954; rev. ed. 1969) and
*Burs under the Saddle: A Second Look at Books and Histories
of the West* (Norman: University of Oklahoma Press, 1964).

To my knowledge, the accuracy of *Robber and Hero* has
never been questioned. In his preface, George Huntington
lists the individuals, including eyewitnesses and participants in the events of September 7, 1876, whom he con-
sulted for "a correct account of the facts involved." In
a somewhat more comprehensive statement, he later
claimed:

> I made an exhaustive study of every available
> source of information concerning the raid, inter-
> viewed every man in Northfield who was present
> at any part of the fray, corresponded with every
> man out of Northfield who had anything to do
> with either the street-fight, the bank-fight or the
> fight and capture in Madelia, and read everything
> that has been published in the newspapers of the
> state.[1]

[1]George Huntington to Sam E. Mitchell, Apr. 26, 1914, William Watts
Folwell Papers, MHS.

A close examination of these same sources, many of which reside in the Minnesota Historical Society's manuscript and newspaper collections, bears out Huntington's claim. Huntington's account is accurate, apart from two minor mistakes of identification: on page 48, he confuses Clel Miller with Bill Stiles, whom Huntington correctly identifies on page 4 as the former Minnesota resident and guide for the outlaw "expedition," and on pages 3 and 75, Sam Wells (the alias of Charles Pitts) is named George Wells.

The only significant error in *Robber and Hero* concerns the identity of the Norwegian lad whose discovery of the Younger brothers and Charlie Pitts led to their capture. Huntington noted in his "Roll of Honor" (pages 99–100) that he had failed to ascertain "any trace of the brave boy who was the Paul Revere of the final victory." There was good reason for this. "Oscar Oleson Suborn," the name known to Huntington and given in all accounts, official and otherwise, was a pseudonym for Asle Oscar Sorbel, who adopted his ficticious name ostensibly for fear of reprisals by other gang members and friends of the Missouri outlaws. It was not until 1929, after a long career as a veterinarian in South Dakota, that Sorbel officially disclosed his true identity and relationship to the events near Madelia in 1876. For most Minnesotans, the newspaper report of Sorbel's death in 1930 was their first news of the secret that had eluded Huntington's documentary net thirty-five years earlier.[2]

[2]*Northfield News*, July 25, 1930, p. 3.

Some explanation also must be given for Huntington's cryptic remarks about the bodies of Stiles and Miller (page 46). Although the story is more complicated than can be told here, the salient points are interesting. It is true that the bodies were quietly buried, almost immediately exhumed, and surreptitiously shipped away to the medical school at the University of Michigan, to be used as cadavers for anatomical instruction. As was typical in the nineteenth century, spare bodies were constantly in short supply and students were often responsible for providing corpses for their own study. The fellow responsible for snatching the bodies of Stiles and Miller was none other than Michigan medical student Henry M. Wheeler, the same resourceful lad whose fusilade from the Dampier Hotel killed Clel Miller and wounded Bob Younger. With the help of two of his Michigan classmates, also Northfield residents, Wheeler arranged for shipment of the illegally exhumed bodies to Ann Arbor in kegs labeled "Fresh Paint." Wheeler retained possession of Miller's skeleton and displayed it in his office in Grand Forks, N.Dak., throughout his lengthy practice. (The skeleton eventually was destroyed in a fire.)

For the record, Wheeler had a distinguished career as a physician and surgeon, attaining distinction as the first dean of the University of North Dakota medical school and first president of North Dakota's state board of medical examiners. He also was elected to two terms as mayor of Grand Forks. For obvious reasons, Huntington determined

that body snatching was a bit more than the reading public
might have tolerated, especially from one of Northfield's il-
lustrious local heroes.[3]

[3]Francis F. McKinney, "The Northfield Raid, and Its Ann Arbor Se-
quel," *Michigan Alumnus Quarterly Review* 61 (Dec. 4, 1954): 38–45; William Holtz, "Bankrobbers, Burkers, and Bodysnatchers," *Michigan Quarterly Review* 6 (Spring 1967): 90–98; Roger Barr, "Others Reap Northfield
Raid Riches," *St. Paul Pioneer Press/Dispatch*, Sept. 5, 1981, p. 12B. On
Wheeler's career, see *Northfield News*, Apr. 18, 1930, p. 1, 3.

PREFACE.

Accounts of bank-robberies and other exploits of outlaws and desperadoes are usually supposed to belong to the criminal-news columns of the daily paper and to the writer of sensational literature. When the robber is the only or the principal actor in the scene, and his prowess or brutality the only feature worth mentioning, the less said of it the better. But when a great crime is the occasion of great heroism, courage, fidelity, intrepid resistance, and the triumph of virtue over violence, then there is a story worth telling, and a lesson worth learning.

It is such a story that is unfolded in the following pages. The attempted robbery of the Northfield bank, the refusal of Mr. Heywood to open the safe, his brutal murder by the baffled robber, the brave and successful fight made by the citizens, the flight, pursuit and capture of the bandits,—all this was familiar enough to the whole nation eighteen years ago. But such

events easily pass from the recollection of men;
while to a generation of young people now growing up it has never been known. To some of us
it has seemed, therefore, that the time has come
to tell the story again, not from the sensational
point of view, but from that of heroism and
loyalty to duty.

The aim of the author has been to give a
correct account of the facts involved, and leave
them to convey their own lesson and inspiration.
Revolting details have been omitted. All important statements are made upon the authority of
eye-witnesses, where such testimony was accessible, and in most cases by the collation of a
number of independent accounts.

The author takes pleasure in acknowledging his
indebtedness for various services and courtesies,
the loan of photographs, the furnishing of information, and many valuable aids and suggestions,
to the following persons among others:—Messrs.
G. M. Phillips, A. R. Manning, F. J. Wilcox, S.
Trussell, H. S. French, Rev. J. W. Strong, D. D.,
and Miss M. J. Evans, of Northfield, Minnesota;
Messrs. W. W. Murphy, C. A. Pomeroy, G. A.
Bradford, W. J. McCarthy, of Madelia, Minnesota; Mr. S. J. Severson, of Brookings, South
Dakota; Col. T. L. Vought and Mr. T. L. Vought,

Jr., of La Crosse, Wisconsin; Mr. A. E. Bunker, of Chicago, Illinois; Dr. H. M. Wheeler, of Grand Forks, North Dakota; Mr. H. M. Serkland, of St. James, Minnesota; Messrs. S. L. Heywood, of Minneapolis, Minnesota, and J. C. Heywood, of Alta, Iowa; Hon. W. D. Rice and G. S. Thompson, Esq., of Sioux City, Iowa; and Marshall W. K. Holmes, of Spokane, Wash. Hearty acknowledgment is also made of the important assistance derived from Rev. D. L. Leonard's funeral discourse on Mr. Heywood, from files of the Pioneer Press and Tribune of the time of the raid, and from the excellent and accurate history of it and its related events, entitled "The Northfield Tragedy," by Mr. John Jay Lemon.

It only remains to say that the book herewith presented to the public is intended both as a memorial of Mr. Heywood and as a tribute to the valor and heroic endeavor of all those who helped or tried to help in resisting, pursuing or capturing his assailants and their confederates. Whatever pecuniary profits may accrue from its sale will be sacredly devoted to the erection of a monument to the memory of Mr. Heywood.

ROBBER AND HERO

THE STORY OF THE RAID

ON THE

FIRST NATIONAL BANK OF NORTHFIELD,

MINNESOTA,

BY THE

JAMES-YOUNGER BAND OF ROBBERS,

IN 1876

THE TRAGEDY IN THE BANK,

THE BATTLE IN THE STREET,

THE TWO-WEEKS PURSUIT,

THE FINAL CAPTURE.

Portraits, Illustrations and Biographical Sketches

Compiled from Original and Authentic Sources

BY GEORGE HUNTINGTON

ROBBER AND HERO.

CHAPTER I.

THE BANDIT SPIES.

In the latter part of August, 1876, a mysterious company of men made their appearance in southern Minnesota, and proceeded to visit various cities and villages in that part of the state. There were certainly eight of them, and possibly nine, some of them hard, vicious-looking fellows, from whom people instinctively shrank, others gentlemanly, handsome, and even imposing in personal appearance. They travelled on horseback and rode like men accustomed to live in the saddle. They had the finest of horses and equipment, part of it brought with them, the rest purchased after they entered the state. They had plenty of money and spent it lavishly. In their progress from place to place they did not go like an organized band, but wandered here and there, sometimes two by two, sometimes four or five together. When several of them visited a town together, they went to different hotels and avoided all appearance of collusion or of common design. Often they avoided towns and sought entertainment at the houses of farmers or other citizens, where they found no difficulty in making themselves agreeable and in giving a plausible account of themselves. Wherever they went, they attracted more or less attention, excited the curiosity of the inquisitive, and occasionally the suspicions of the wary; but upon most people they made the impression of well-bred respectability. They passed for civil engineers looking up railway routes, for capitalists in search of land, for stockmen dealing in horses and cattle. Their outfit and mode of travel made either of these suppositions reasonable, and their smooth courtesy, affability and apparent frankness were accepted in lieu of credentials of character. That they were not all that they pretended to be many people suspected; but that they were a band of outlaws, or rather a combination of three bands, comprising the most notorious desperadoes in the country, laying their plans for a great robbery, no one suspected. Still less did they themselves suspect that their career of crime was so near its close, or that they were making deliberate plans for their own destruction.

Of course they passed under assumed names, introducing themselves as J. C. King, Jack Ward, etc. It is now known that the band consisted of the following men: Jesse James and his brother Frank, Thomas C. Younger (commonly known as Cole Younger) and his brothers James and Robert, Clel Miller, William Stiles, alias Chadwell, and Charles Pitts, alias Geo. Wells. Some persons maintain that there was a ninth man, but he has never been identified, and is commonly believed to be mythical. The eight whose names are given were all men of criminal antecedents, and some of them with a record for deeds of the most revolting atrocity; though several of them were connected with highly respectable families.

In prospecting for a favorable opening, they visited a number of places, going as far north as St. Paul and Minneapolis, and as far east as Red Wing. In each place they made a careful study of the chances for successful operations in their line and of routes of escape, visiting the banks on one pretext or another, and familiarizing themselves with all facts that had any bearing on their scheme. They took special pains to make them-

selves acquainted with such features of the
country as would aid or hinder them in going
and coming on their intended raid; as, for
instance, the location of lakes, streams, swamps
or forests, on the one hand, and that of roads,
bridges and fords, on the other. The situation
and the resources of villages, the extent of country
population, and the nationality and character of
the people also interested them. With the aid of
maps, printed statements and minute inquiries,
they succeeded in gaining a large amount of
information, without betraying their purpose,—
information which they found exceedingly con-
venient at a later day. They also had the
advantage of being to a certain extent person-
ally conducted. Stiles, one of their number, had
formerly lived in Rice county, and was therefore
able to act as a sort of guide for the expedition,
if, indeed, he was not, as some think, its instigator. Their reliance upon him, however, proved in
the end, as we shall see, a source of danger rather
than of safety.

Finding nothing to their mind in the great
cities, they turned their attention to a group of
country towns lying farther south, including
St. Peter, Mankato, Lake Crystal, Madelia, St.
James, Garden City, Janesville, Cordova, Water-

ville, Millersburg, Cannon City and Northfield. These, again, divide themselves into two smaller groups, having direct or indirect relation to the two points of attack selected by the robbers, and all of them being on or near a diagonal line, extending about thirty or forty miles southwest and about forty or fifty miles northeast of Mankato.

Having completed their preliminary survey, they prepared for their grand exploit. Their first project was the robbery of one or more of the banks of Mankato, a thriving town at the great bend of the Minnesota River. Five of the band appeared in Mankato on Saturday, September 2nd, and, as usual, created a sensation with their fine horses and horsemanship. They made purchases at some of the stores, and paid a visit to the First National Bank, where they got change for a fifty-dollar bill. According to their custom, they stayed at different hotels, at least four of them did, while the fifth sought some other resort not identified. On Sunday night two of them were known to be at a notorious resort on the opposite side of the river, a rendezvous of the lowest criminals, where, as is believed, they were in consultation with confederates with reference to their intended raid and subsequent escape.

Meantime, Jesse James had been recognized by a man who knew him by sight, and the fact was reported to the police who shadowed the men until midnight, and put some of the bank people on their guard against possible burglaries; though no one anticipated an open attack by daylight.

On Monday, the 4th, the robbers mounted their horses and rode forth to their intended attack. Their plan was to make it about noon, when the bank force would be reduced and the streets would be most free of citizens. They had already arrived opposite the First National Bank, when they noticed a number of citizens on the sidewalk, and saw one of them apparently calling another's attention to the approaching horsemen. The robbers, fearing that they were suspected and watched, deferred the attack till a later hour. On returning, however, they saw the same citizens again, seeming, as before, to be keeping close watch upon the strangers. Convinced now that their purpose was discovered and that the citizens were prepared for them, the robbers abandoned their project and left Mankato as speedily as possible. The truth was that they were at that moment the object of no suspicion whatever. The regular weekly meeting of the Board of

Trade, and some repairs on an adjoining building, had called together the unusual number of persons whom the robbers observed, and the man who was supposed to be directing his companion's attention to the bandits was simply remarking upon the fine quality of their horses. No doubt, however, the presence of so large a number of spectators would have seriously embarrassed the gang in beginning operations. As it was, they served just as good a purpose in repelling the attack as if they had been a company of armed militia on duty.

CHAPTER II.

Abandoning Mankato, the robbers now moved upon Northfield as directly as roads and available stopping-places would permit. Monday night found them in Janesville, eighteen miles east of Mankato; Tuesday night in Cordova, about the same distance north of Janesville; Wednesday night in Millersburg, northeast of Cordova. The rest of the band spent the same Wednesday night in Cannon City. Millersburg is eleven miles west of Northfield, Cannon City ten miles south.

Northfield is a quiet but enterprising little city, in the heart of a rich and well cultivated agricultural region which is tributary to it. It has good railroad facilities; and the Cannon River, flowing through the town, affords power for its mills and adds a picturesque feature to its scenery. A bridge crosses the river in the centre of the town, connecting its eastern and its western divisions, and leading, on the eastern side, into an open space known as Bridge Square, where many of the stores are to be found. On the eastern side of the Square runs Division Street, the principal business street of the city, along the foot of a bluff some fifty feet in height, ascended by various streets, and crowned with residences, churches and educational buildings. Prominent among the public edifices are those of Carleton College, in the northeastern part of the city; while St. Olaf surmounts a high eminence in the northwestern. An observant stranger, entering the city for the first time, could hardly fail to get the impression of intelligence, thrift and commercial enterprise. This was precisely the impression made upon the robbers; and it was this impression which led them to select Northfield as a field of operations.

Ten or twelve days before the final attempt upon the bank, two members of the band had visited the town for a preliminary survey. They conversed with citizens, as their custom was, making inquiries about roads, etc., particularly about the route to Mankato, and awakened the suspicion of at least one or two of the citizens as to the truth of their pretensions. They found a bank doing a large business, and presumably carrying a large volume of cash; and they saw the people quiet and industrious, and presumably neither prepared nor disposed to meet force with force. What plans they then formed for the subsequent raid it is impossible to say; but it is certain that they were no sooner foiled in Mankato than they started for Northfield.

As we have already seen, the two divisions of the band spent the night of Wednesday, September 6th, in neighboring villages, within easy reach of their next day's destination. Early on the morning of Thursday, the 7th, they took up their march along the roads converging upon Northfield, meeting in the woods west of the town. In the course of the forenoon, some of them appeared upon the streets and in the stores, where two of them were recognized as the same two that had made the previous visit of inspection already referred to. They all wore linen dusters, a garment much more common with the traveler in those days than in our own, and one that seemed entirely suitable for the sultry weather then prevailing, while it served to conceal the pistols and cartridge-belts, with which the robbers were so liberally supplied. Five of the men dined together at a restaurant on the west side of the river, waiting contentedly for their dinner to be cooked, conversing with the proprietor on politics and other indifferent subjects, and, after they had finished their meal, still delaying unaccountably, probably to give time for the arrival of the rest of their accomplices. Finally they remounted their horses and rode over the bridge.

It is difficult, and, so far as the present writer is concerned, impossible, after the most painstaking study of all available sources of information, to determine the exact order of events at the opening of the attack. No one observer followed all the preliminary movements of the robbers. One person noticed one thing and another another; and each depended more or less upon hearsay for items not within his personal knowledge. The similarity of dress already referred to made it difficult to distinguish the robbers from one another; while the wild excitement which soon ensued gave little opportunity for careful observation. With no attempt to reconcile conflicting statements, therefore, which happily differ only in unimportant details, this narrative will confine itself to those facts upon which all witnesses agree.

The scene of the robbery and the movements of the robbers may be easily understood from the accompanying cut. The center of operations was the corner of Bridge Square and Division Street. On this corner stood a two-story stone building known as the Scriver Block. Its upper story was used for offices, and was reached by an outside stairway on Division Street. The larger part of the lower story was occupied by two stores, ranging north and south, and having their front entrances on the northern or Bridge Square side. At the extreme southern end of the building, and having its entrance on the eastern or Division Street side, was the object of attack—the First National Bank. On the western side of the block ran a narrow alley, affording rear entrances to the stores and the bank. West of the alley, and fronting on the square, were two hardware stores whose respective proprietors were leading actors in the scene that followed,—J. S. Allen and A. R. Manning. On the eastern side of Division Street, opposite the Scriver Block, were a hotel and a number of stores, in front of one of which stood a young man who was also to have a prominent part in the coming affray,—Mr. H. M. Wheeler, then at home on a vacation from his medical studies in Michigan University.

As has been previously stated, the robber band comprised three subdivisions,—the two James brothers, the three Younger brothers, and three odd ones,—Miller, Pitts and Stiles. In their active operations another threefold division was adopted, each of the squads containing one of the Younger brothers and one of the odd ones, and two of them containing one of the James brothers. That is there were two trios and one couple. Of these, one trio was detailed to commit the robbery, while the couple co-operated with them on Division Street, and the other trio acted as a rear guard on Bridge Square, the direction in which the band intended to retreat.

It was about 2 o'clock in the afternoon that the first trio, consisting of Pitts, Bob Younger and, it is believed, one of the James brothers, came over the bridge, and crossing the Square from northwest to southeast, dismounted in front of the bank, throwing their bridle reins over some hitching-posts beside the street. They then sauntered to the corner and lounged upon some dry-goods boxes in front of the store (Lee and Hitchcock's) assuming an air of indifference, and whittling the boxes, like the most commonplace loafers. Presently the two horsemen constituting the second detail entered Division Street from the south, and rode toward the bank. They were Cole Younger and Clel Miller. Upon their approach the three men at the corner walked back to the door of the bank and went in. Miller, dismounting in front of the door, left his horse unhitched, went to the door and looked in, and then, closing it, walked back and forth before it. Younger dismounted in the middle of the street, where he made a pretense of tightening his saddle-girth.

By this time the attention of several citizens had been attracted to the maneuvers of the robbers. Word had been brought that nine men on horseback had been seen coming out of the woods southwest of the city; and the presence of so many strange horsemen on the street began to awaken uneasiness. Yet when some expressed these fears, they were laughed at by others, and assured that the men were merely cattle-buyers on a legitimate business tour.

Among those whose suspicions had been especially aroused were Dr. Wheeler and Mr. J. S. Allen, already referred to. Dr. Wheeler was sitting under an awning in front of his father's store on the east side of Division Street when the men entered the street; and as their actions seemed to him to indicate some mischievous intent, he rose and moved along the sidewalk till he was opposite them. Mr. Allen was on the other side of the street; and when he saw the three men enter the bank, he attempted to follow them in. He was instantly seized by Miller, who had been placed there for that purpose, and who, drawing his revolver, and pouring forth a volley of oaths, ordered Allen to stand back, and warned him on peril of his life not to utter a word. Allen jerked away from the ruffian's grasp, and ran back to and around the corner toward his store, shouting in a voice that resounded blocks away, "Get your guns, boys! They're robbing the bank!" At the same time Dr. Wheeler had stepped into the street, and was shouting, "Robbery! Robbery!" his alarm being at once justified and intensified by the sound of pistol shots within the bank.

Upon this, Miller and Younger sprang into their saddles, ordering Wheeler back, with oaths and threats, and firing one or two shots over his head, to intimidate him and to give notice to their confederates that their game was discovered. Then the two robbers began riding up and down Division Street, at their utmost speed, shooting right and left, and with horrible oaths calling upon every one they saw to "get in"—an order that was obeyed with pretty general promptness and unanimity. At the same time the three men near the bridge took up the same tactics, and came dashing across the Square, shooting and shouting like their comrades, whom they joined on Division Street. Wherever they saw a head,

out of doors or at a window, they sent a shower
of balls. The air was filled with the sounds of
the fray,—the incessant bang bang of the heavy
revolvers, the whistling of bullets, the crashing of
glass and the chorus of wild yells and imprecations. The first intention of the robbers was not
to kill any one, but to strike terror into the minds
of the people, and, by driving everybody from the
streets, to give the men in the bank time to work,
to prevent any attempt at interference, and to
secure themselves an unobstructed line of retreat.
Strange to say, during this part of the affray,
though the robbers kept up a constant fusilade
from their revolvers, but one person was shot,—a
Scandinavian who could not understand English,
and who was fatally wounded while persistently
remaining on the street.

CHAPTER III.

Meantime, a very different scene was enacted within the bank, where the first trio of robbers were dealing with a trio of bank employes as resolute as themselves. These were Mr. A. E. Bunker, teller, Mr. J. L. Heywood, book-keeper and Mr. F. J. Wilcox, assistant book-keeper. The cashier, Mr. G. M. Phillips, being out of the state, Mr. Heywood was acting cashier. The bank was at the time occupying temporary quarters, not arranged with reference to emergencies of this kind. A counter, constructed somewhat like an ordinary office or store counter, extended across two sides, between the lobby and the interior of the room. This was surmounted for nearly its entire length by a high railing containing glass panels; but in the angle between the two sections of the counter there was an open space, entirely unprotected, wide enough for a man to pass through.

When the three robbers entered the bank the

employés were busy at their tasks, and had no suspicion of approaching danger. Mr. Bunker, the teller, hearing footsteps in the lobby, and supposing that some customer had entered, turned from his work to wait upon him, coming to the open space before referred to. There three revolvers were pointing at him, and he was peremptorily ordered to throw up his hands. His first impression was that some of his friends were playing a practical joke upon him. Before he had time to comprehend the situation, the three robbers had climbed over the counter, and covering him and his associates with their revolvers, commanded them to hold up their hands.

"We're going to rob this bank," said one of the men. "Don't any of you holler. We've got forty men outside." Then, with a flourish of his revolver, he pointed to Heywood and said, "Are you the cashier?"

"No," replied Heywood.

The same question was put to Bunker and to Wilcox, each of whom made the same reply.

"You are the cashier," said the robber, turning upon Heywood, who was sitting at the cashier's desk, and who appeared to be the oldest of the employes. "Open that safe —— quick, or I'll blow your head off."

A second robber—Pitts—then ran to the vault
and stepped inside, whereupon Heywood, who
had risen to his feet, followed him and attempted
to close the door. He was instantly dragged
back, and the two robbers, thrusting their revolvers in his face, said, "Open that safe, now, or you
havn't but a minute to live," accompanying their
threats with oaths.

"There is a time lock on," Heywood replied,
"and it cannot be opened now."

"That's a lie!" retorted the robbers, again repeatedly demanding, with threats and profanity,
that the safe be opened, and dragging Heywood
roughly about the room.

Finally, seeming to realize what desperate men
he was dealing with, Heywood shouted, "Murder!
Murder! Murder!" Whereupon one of the robbers struck him a terrible blow on the head with
a revolver, felling him to the floor. Pitts then
drew a knife from his pocket, and opening it, said,
"Let's cut his —— throat," and made a feint of
doing so, inflicting a slight wound on Heywood's
neck as he lay helpless upon the floor. The two
men then dragged him from where he lay, at the
rear of his desk, back to the door of the vault,
still demanding that he open the safe. Occasionally also they turned from him to Bunker and

Wilcox, pointing their revolvers at them and calling on them to "Unlock that safe." To this demand the young men answered that they could not unlock the safe. The statement was true, though in a sense quite different from that in which the robbers understood it. The reason that they could not unlock it was that it was unlocked already. The door was closed and the bolts were shot into place, but the combination dial was not turned. This was one of the humors of the situation, but one which those in the secret were not in a position to enjoy. As a last resort for coercing Heywood, who was still lying on the floor, in but a partially conscious condition, Pitts placed his revolver close to Heywood's head and fired. The bullet passed into the vault and through a tin box containing jewelry and papers left by some customer for safe keeping. This was the first shot fired in the bank, and its futility well foretokened the failure of the whole effort.

While Bunker and Wilcox received occasional attention from Heywood's assailants, their special custodian was Bob Younger. As Bunker had his pen in his hand when first ordered to hold up his hands, it remained for a time poised in the air, when he made an effort to lay it down. Younger, noticing the movement, and thinking it an attempt to reach a weapon, sprang at Bunker, and thrusting his revolver into his face, said, "Here, put up your hands and keep 'em up, or I'll kill you!" Then, to hold his prisoners more completely under his control, he compelled them both to get down on their knees under the counter. All the robbers were very much excited, and increasingly so as they found themselves baffled and resisted. Younger would point his pistol first at one of the young men and then at the other, turning from time to time to search among the papers on the desk, or to open a drawer in quest of valuables.

While still on his knees, Bunker remembered a revolver kept on a shelf under the teller's window, and edged toward the place in hope of reaching it. Turning his head that way while Younger's back was toward him, his movement was instantly detected by Pitts, who leaped before him, and seizing the pistol, put it in his own pocket, remarking, "You needn't try to get hold of that. You couldn't do any thing with that little derringer, anyway." It is no doubt fortunate that Bunker did not succeed in reaching the weapon, as he would almost certainly have been shot down by the robbers before he could use it. The pistol was found upon Pitts at the time of his capture and death.

Bunker now rose to his feet, intending to make some effort to escape or to give an alarm. As he did so, Younger turned to him and said, "Where's the money outside the safe? Where's the cashier's till?" Bunker showed him a partitioned box on the counter, containing some small change and fractional currency; but did not call his attention to a drawer beneath the counter, containing $3,000 in bills. Again ordering Bunker to get down on his knees and keep his hands up, Younger drew from under his coat a grain-sack, which he began to fill from the box. Presently he turned again to Bunker, and finding him on his feet, he said, with a wicked look and with an outburst of horrible profanity, "There's more money than that out here. Where's that cashier's till? And what in —— are you standing up for? I told you to keep down." Seizing Bunker, and forcing him to the floor, Younger pressed the muzzle of his revolver against Bunker's temple and said, "Show me where that money is, you —— —— —— or I'll kill you!" Receiving no answer, he left Bunker and renewed his search for the money.

Bunker once more regained his feet, and taking advantage of a moment when the robber's face was turned, he dashed past Wilcox, into and through the directors' room, to the rear door, then closed with blinds fastened on the inside. His intention was to enter the rear of Manning's hardware store, on the other side of the alley, and give the alarm. He knew nothing yet of what was going on in the street, and he believed Heywood to be dead from the effect of the pistol shot apparently aimed at his head.

The first of the robbers to notice the escape was Pitts, whose eyes seemed to be everywhere at once, and who was then with Heywood in front of the vault. Before he had time to shoot, however, Bunker was out of his range around the corner of the vault, and making for the door. With a mad yell Pitts bounded after the fugitive, and coming in sight of him, fired as he ran, the ball whizzing past Bunker's ear and through the blind in front of him. Bunker threw his weight against the blinds, bursting them open, plunged down a flight of outside steps, and had nearly reached the rear entrance of the next building when he was again fired upon by Pitts. This time the ball hit its mark, passing through the right shoulder, near the joint, barely missing the sub-clavian artery, and coming out just below the collar-bone. As he felt the sting and shock of the wound, he stumbled; but keeping his feet, and not knowing how badly he might be wounded, he ran on across a vacant lot and around to a surgeon's office in the next block. Pitts gave up the chase and returned to his companions in the bank, but only to hear one of their confederates on the outside shout, "The game is up! Better get out, boys. They're killing all our men." Hearing this, the three robbers sprang through the teller's window and rushed into the street. As the last one climbed over the counter, he turned toward poor Heywood, who had gotten upon his feet and was staggering toward his desk, and deliberately shot him through the head. The act was without provocation or excuse, and was afterwards denounced by others of the gang as "a fool act," though others still made an absurd attempt to justify it on the ground of self-defense. It was a piece of cowardly revenge on the part of a ruffian who was made desperate by defeat, and who, as was evident throughout the entire scene in the bank. was badly under the influence of liquor.

CHAPTER IV.

ON THE STREET.

The battle in the street was now at its height, and the spirit in which it was waged on the part of the citizens showed how grossly the robbers had mistaken the mettle of the people with whom they had to deal. The community was taken by surprise and at a great disadvantage. It was at the height of the prairie-chicken season, and a majority of the men who had guns were away in the field. The excellent hunting in the neighborhood had drawn many sportsmen from the larger cities, accustoming the people to the presence of strangers, while they had no reason to expect a hostile invasion. When the mounted bandits on Bridge Square and Division Street began riding and shooting, the first impression was that of surprise. Some thought it the reckless fun of drunken scapegraces. Some took the riders to be the attaches of a traveling show, advertising their performance. When the bullets began to fly about people's ears, and the character of the invaders became evident, every body was stunned and dazed, and there was a general scramble for shelter. But the next moment there was an equally prompt rally of brave men to repel the attack.

Dr. Wheeler, who had been one of the first to give the alarm, and who had been driven from the street by the imprecations and bullets of the robbers, hastened to the drug-store where he usually kept his gun. Remembering as he went that he had left it at the house, he did not slacken his pace, but kept on through the store, heading first for the house of a neighbor, where he hoped a weapon might be found, but on second thought turning into the Dampier Hotel, close at hand, where he remembered to have seen one. There, instead of the fowling-piece he looked for, he found an old army carbine, for which, with the help of Mr. Dampier the clerk, three cartridges were discovered in another part of the house. All this was so quickly done, that he was at a second-story chamber window, with his gun loaded, in time for the beginning of the fight.

Meantime Mr. Allen, who had also sounded so prompt and vigorous an alarm, ran to his store where he had a number of guns, and loading them

with such ammunition as came to his hand, gave
them to anybody who would take them. One of
them was taken by Mr. Elias Stacy, who used it
to good purpose in the battle that followed.

As Mr. Allen went to his own store, he had
passed that of Mr. Manning, to whom he shouted
his warning concerning the robbers. Up to this
time Manning had no suspicion of what was
going on. One of the robbers had been in the
store in the forenoon, looking about and pretend-
ing he wanted to buy a gun. He was a genteel,
well-dressed fellow, and Manning supposed him to
be some stranger who had come to Northfield to
hunt; though he did not believe that he wanted
any gun, and thought there was something wrong
about him. Even when the three horsemen dashed
through the Square so noisily and belligerently, he
thought little of it. But when he heard Allen's
shout, and made out the words "Robbing the
Bank," he recalled what he had seen and the
meaning of it all flashed upon his mind. Abruptly
leaving the customer he was serving, he rushed for
a weapon, thinking hard and fast. Pistols? No,
they would be of little account. His shotgun?
Yes—No; he had left all his loaded cartridges at
home. His breach-loading rifle! That was the
thing; and here it was in the window; and there

in a pigeon-hole of his desk were the cartridges, where they had been carelessly thrown months before. All this came to him without an instant's loss of time. He forgot nothing and he made no mistakes. Stripping the rifle of its cover, and seizing a handful of cartridges, he hurried to the scene of battle, loading as he ran

The scene on the street is indescribable. People had not only made haste to get out of the way of the leaden hail-storm that had burst forth, but had also taken measures to protect themselves and their property against the raiders, whose intention was believed to be not only to rob the bank but to pillage the entire town. Stores and offices were hastily closed. The postmaster, Capt. H. S. French, who chanced to have an exceptionally heavy registered mail on hand that day, hastened to lock it in the safe and close the Office. Jewelers and others who had valuable and portable stock pursued a similar course. The news of the invasion, emphasized by the sound of the shooting, spread swiftly through the town. Warning was sent to the public school and to Carleton College to keep the students off the streets. The general impression was that the town was in possession of a horde of robbers, numbering nobody knew how many, and coming nobody knew whence, and bent on ruthless plunder, nobody knew to what extent.

The scene of the actual conflict was that part of Division Street on which the bank faced, and scarcely a full block in length. Here the five mounted robbers were riding back and forth, up one side of the street and down the other, doing their utmost with voice and arms to keep up the reign of terror which they had begun. The citizens whom they had driven in were looking for weapons, and the bolder ones were coming back, some armed and some unarmed, around the margin of the field. Capt. French, having made Uncle Sam's property as secure as possible, stood in front of the locked door, wondering where he could soonest find a gun. Justice Streater and ex policeman Elias Hobbs stepped out into the Square, empty handed but undaunted, and determined to do something by way of resistance to the invasion. A few were so fortunate as to have not only the courage but the means for an armed defence. Mr. Stacy, already referred to, came out with a fowling-piece, and confronting Miller, just as the latter was mounting his horse, fired at his head. The fine bird shot marked the robber's face, and the force of the charge knocked him back from the saddle, but inflicted no serious wound.

There was a poetic justice in the incident, as it was Allen, whom Miller had seized and threatened at the bank, who owned and loaded the gun, and sent it out in the hands of his neighbor to draw first blood from the very man that had assaulted its owner.

Later on in the battle Messrs. J. B. Hyde, Ross Phillips and James Gregg also did their best with similar weapons, and it was not their fault that the shotguns they used upon the bandits were inadequate to the occasion. Mr. Hobbs, who had no weapon at all, fell back upon more primitive methods, and at the height of the fray came on shouting, "Stone 'em! Stone 'em!" and suiting the action to the word, and choosing not "smooth stones from the brook," but big and formidable missiles, more fit for the hand of Goliath than for the sling of David, hurled rocks and curses at the enemy, and not without effect. Col. Streater also joined in this mode of warfare, which, if not the most effective, certainly evinced as high a degree of courage as they could have shown in the use of the most approved weapons. Other citizens, too, took a hand in the affair, as opportunity offered, and some of them had narrow escapes from the bullets with which the robbers responded to their attentions.

But while there was no lack of good intentions on the part of others, it was the two men with rifles, Manning and Wheeler, who were able to do real execution upon the enemy, and finally to put them to rout. We go back, therefore, to the moment when Manning came running from his store with the rifle in his hand. Taking in the situation at a glance, and intent only upon getting at the robbers, he stepped out into the open street, and amid a shower of bullets, coolly looked for his game. Before him stood the horses of the men who were still in the bank, and over the backs of the horses he saw the heads of two men, upon whom he instantly drew a bead. The men ducked behind the horses, whereupon Manning, without lowering his gun, changed his aim and shot the nearest horse, rightly judging that this would cripple the band almost as effectually as shooting the men. He then dropped back around the corner to reload; but finding to his chagrin that the breach-lever would not throw out the empty shell, he was obliged to go back to the store and get a ramrod with which to dislodge it, thus losing valuable time. The interruption proved a good thing for him, however, moderating his excitement and rashness, and preparing him to do better execution. Soon he was at the corner again. Peering around the corner, he saw one of the robbers between the horses and the bank door, and fired at him. The ball grazed the edge of a post, deflecting it slightly; but it found Cole Younger, wounding him in a vulnerable though not vital place. Again Manning dropped back to reload. The shell gave him no trouble this time, and he was quickly at his post once more. As he looked cautiously around the corner, he saw Stiles sitting on his horse, some seventy-five or eighty yards away, apparently doing sentry duty in that part of the street. Manning took deliberate aim at him—so deliberate as to excite the impatience and call forth the protests of some who were near him—and fired, shooting the man through the heart. Manning, as before, stepped back to reload, the robber fell from his saddle, dead, and the horse ran to a livery-stable around the corner.

While these things were going on, Dr. Wheeler was not idle. His first shot was at the head of Jim Younger, who was riding by. The gun carried high, and the ball struck the ground beyond him. Younger looked first at the spot where it struck, and then turned to see where it came from, but did not discover the sharp-shooter at the window above him. Wheeler's next shot was at Clel Miller, whom Stacy had already peppered with bird-shot. The bullet passed through his body almost precisely as Pitts' bullet had passed through Bunker's; but in this case the great artery was severed and almost instant death ensued. Wheeler's third and last cartridge had fallen upon the floor, bursting the paper of which it was made, and spilling the powder. Hurrying in search of more, he met his friend Dampier coming with a fresh supply.

The robbers were now badly demoralized. Their shooting had been wild and fruitless. They had lost two men and a horse killed; a third man was wounded; two riderless horses had escaped from them, and an armed force had cut off their proposed line of retreat. It was at this juncture that Cole Younger rode to the door of the bank and shouted to the men inside to come out, which they made all haste to do. Two of the men mounted their horses, which still stood before the door. There was no horse for Bob Younger, and he was compelled to fight on foot.

By this time Manning and Wheeler had both reloaded, and returned to their places. As Manning showed himself, ready to renew the battle, Bob Younger came running toward him down the sidewalk. Manning raised his rifle to shoot at the

approaching robber, and at the same instant
Younger drew his revolver to shoot Manning. In
the effort to get out of each other's range,
Younger dodged under the outside stairway of
the Scriver Block, while Manning stood at the
corner beyond it. The stairs were thus between
them, and neither of them could get a shot at the
other without exposing himself to the fire of his
adversary. For a time they kept up a game of
hide and seek, each trying in vain to catch the
other off his guard and get the first shot. At
this point Wheeler, though he could but imper-
fectly see Younger's body beneath the stair, took
a shot at him. The ball struck the robber's elbow,
shattering the bone. He then coolly changed his
pistol to his left hand and continued his efforts to
shoot Manning.

It then occurred to Manning that by running
around through the store he might reach the street
on the other side of the robber, and so drive
him from his hiding-place. This plan he instantly
put in execution. At the same moment Wheeler
was engaged in reloading his gun. But the
robbers had their plans, too, and took advantage
of this momentary lull to make their escape. Bob
Younger sprang from his hiding-place and ran
up Division street, where he mounted behind his

brother Cole; and the entire band,—or at least
what was left of it,—turned and fled. Wheeler
returned to his window and Manning emerged
upon the sidewalk only to find that their game
had flown. Even then there was an excellent
chance for long-range shooting; but the interven-
ing space was immediately filled with people,
making it impossible to shoot without endanger-
ing innocent lives.

This battle between desperados and peaceful
citizens has well been cited as proof that the
prowess, courage and dead-shot skill at arms
commonly ascribed to the border ruffian are
largely imaginary. On the one side was a band
of heavily armed and thoroughly trained and
organized banditti, carrying out a carefully made
plan, in their own line of business, after weeks of
preparation. On the other side was a quiet, law-
abiding community, unused to scenes of violence,
taken utterly by surprise and at a fearful disadvantage, with no adequate means of defence
except two long-disused rifles in out-of-the-way
places, and one of them on the retired army list.
Yet the banditti were beaten at their own game,
and their courage lasted only while the odds were
in their favor. As to marksmanship, they were
vastly outdone by their citizen opponents. Ex-

cepting the cold-blooded murder of a defenceless spectator, they did not in the entire fight fire one effective shot. It is said that at least thirty shots were fired at Manning alone; yet he escaped without a scratch.

In the bank, heroism of another order had displayed itself. Without the excitement of open battle, or the stimulus of numbers, and without the slightest means or opportunity for defence, the three unarmed young men balked the three armed ruffians who held them in their power, meeting threats and violence with passive resistance, and in the face of death itself refusing to yield one jot to the demands of their assailants.

The brunt of this unequal contest fell upon poor Heywood. How he met it has been already related. Threatened, assaulted, dragged about, brutally struck down, menaced with the knife, ostensibly shot at, he could not be persuaded or bullied into surrendering his trust or becoming the accomplice of robbers. It is interesting to know that before this ordeal came to him he had been led to ask himself what he would do in such an emergency, and had made up his mind that he would under no circumstances give up the property of his employers. His steadfast resistance to the robbers' demands, therefore, was not due to a hesitating policy, or to the mere obstinate impulse of the moment, but was the result of a deliberate purpose and conviction of duty. The fatal cost of his fidelity was something which he could not have failed to take account of all along, as the most probable end of a struggle with such desperate men as he was dealing with. At a time when we hear so often that persons in similar circumstances have been compelled to unlock vaults or to open safes at the dictation of robbers, there is a wholesome tonic in the example of a man who proved that there is not in the whole world of criminal force a power that can overcome one brave man who chooses at all hazards to do his duty.

CHAPTER V.

The battle was over. So swift had been its movement, so rapidly had its events followed one another, that it was done before people beyond its immediate vicinity knew that it had begun. From its opening to its closing shot it had occupied but seven minutes. But it had been as decisive as it was brief. The object of the attack had failed. The funds of the bank were intact. Six of the robbers were in flight, two of them wounded. In front of the bank lay the dead horse, the first victim of the fight. Near by was the body of Clel Miller, and a half-block away, on the other side of the street, that of Stiles. Of the three deaths, that of the horse alone moved the pity of the spectators. On every hand were shattered windows, the work of the vicious revolvers; while hitching posts, doors, window-frames and store-fronts were scored with bullets. Heywood lay on the bank-floor, where he had fallen at the post of duty. Bunker was in the hands of the surgeons. All the bells of the town had been set ringing. People came hurrying to the scene from every direction. Excited preparations were making to pursue the escaping robbers.

The scenes that followed showed that there were heroines as well as heroes in the community. While the first wild rumors of the affair were rife, and it was believed that scores of marauders had invaded the town, and that general pillage might be expected, ladies went to the public school and to the girls' dormitory of Carleton College, to give warning of the impending danger. One of the teachers in the public school was the wife of Mr. Bunker, the wounded teller. From different sources she received information first that he was wounded and then that he was killed. Crediting the least alarming statement, she first made arrangements for the care of her pupils, and then started to find her husband. Fortunately she met a friend with a carriage, who took her to the doctor's office where Mr. Bunker was receiving surgical care.

Mrs. Heywood's first intimation of her husband's death was received by accident, and in a painfully abrupt manner. Being at her house on the west side of the river, at a considerable dis-

tance from the scene of the tragedy, she chanced
to hear one neighbor shout the news to another
across the street. President Strong of Carleton
College had already started at the request of
friends, to break the intelligence to her, when he
learned that his errand was needless. The body
was placed in a carriage and supported in the
arms of President Strong, while it was driven to
the Heywood residence. Mrs. Heywood showed
herself worthy to be the wife of such a man. She
bore the awful blow with the greatest calmness;
and when she heard how he met his death, she
said, "I would not have had him do otherwise."

The dead robbers received attentions of quite
another sort. The two bodies were placed in an
empty granary, where they remained during the
night. The news of the raid had been telegraphed
all over the country; and the evening trains
brought crowds of curious people, eager to see
and hear everything pertaining to the affair. The
next day the number of visitors was so largely
increased and the desire to see the dead bandits
was so great, that the bodies were brought out
into the open square, which was soon packed with
people. Among the visitors from other towns were
sheriffs, police officers and private citizens who
had come to join in the pursuit of the escaped
robbers.

That afternoon the county coroner, Dr. Waugh of Faribault, held an inquest on the three bodies, and a verdict was found according to the facts: "That J. L. Heywood came to his death by a pistol-shot fired by an unknown man who was attempting to rob the First National Bank of Northfield;" "That the two unknown men came to their death by the discharge of firearms in the hands of our citizens in self-defence, and in protecting the property of the First National Bank of Northfield."

The grief and indignation over the death of Mr. Heywood were intense. He was a man greatly respected in the community, was prominent in church and business life, and at the time of his death was the City Treasurer and also the Treasurer of Carleton College.

On Sunday, the 10th of September, two funeral services in honor of the murdered man were held in Northfield. In the morning came the public service in High-School Hall, the largest auditorium in the city. The place was packed, notwithstanding the excessive rain and mud then prevailing. The introductory exercises were conducted by the Rev. Messrs. Gossard and Utter, the pastors of the Methodist and the Baptist churches, and the funeral address was

delivered by the Rev. D. L. Leonard, pastor of
the Congregational Church, the regular church
services of the day being omitted. The admirable
address of Mr. Leonard has been preserved in
a neat pamphlet, entitled, "Funeral Discourse on
Joseph Lee Heywood," published by Johnson and
Smith, Minneapolis, and is a valuable contribution
to the literature of this subject. As much of
its biographical and historical matter is substan-
tially covered by the present narrative, it need not
be reproduced ; but some extracts relating to
Mr. Heywood's personal character may properly
be quoted, as showing the estimation in which he
was held by one who not only knew him well, but
was voicing the sentiments of the community to
which and for which he spoke.

"Mr. Heywood was, beyond most men, modest
and timid. He shrank from the public gaze; and,
considering his high gifts and his standing in the
community, he was retiring almost to a fault.
He set a low estimate upon himself. He would
not own to himself, did not even seem to know,
that he was lovable and well-beloved. He courted
no praise and sought no reward. Honors must
come to him unsought if they came at all.
He would be easily content to toil on, out of sight
and with services unrecognized, but in every

transaction he must be conscientious through and through, and do each hour to the full the duties of the hour."

"Yes, something such a one as this walked our streets, worshipped in our assemblies, and bore his share of our public burdens, for ten years. And so dull is human appreciation, that had he ended his days after the ordinary fashion of humanity, it is to be feared his worth had never been widely known. But not so now, since, as I may almost say, in the sight of thousands he has been translated that he should not see death, and was caught up from earth to heaven as in a chariot of fire. Surely we cannot forget that spectacle to our dying day. The glory of his departure will cast back a halo of glory over all his career. We shall re-read the record, as he made it, with sharpened vision. Besides, some of the virtues in which he excelled, such as integrity, moral courage, steadfastness in pursuing the right, in the tragic circumstances attending the close of his life, found their supreme test not only, but their sublime climax as well. The charm lies in the perfect harmony existing between the acts of the last hour and the conduct of all the life that went before.

"And sure am I that we all, in moments when

we are most calm and rational, and when the
noblest in us finds voice, discover the conviction
possessing us that there was something most
fitting, something surpassingly beautiful, in such
an exit after such a career,—such a sunset after
such a day.

"For, for what, I pray you, was man made but
to do his duty? to be brave and true, reckless of
results? And what is life worth, I wonder, if to
be preserved only at the price of cowardice and
faithlessness? . . . Surely to him that is gone
life as the purchase of dishonor would have been
an intolerable burden. . . . Whoso consents to
stand on duty, in the army, on the railway train,
in the banking-house or store, must do it with
open eyes, ready to take the consequences, fully
determined, whatever befall, to play the man.
. . . When so many are corrupt and venal, are
base and criminal in the discharge of public duties,
the spectacle of such a life as we have looked upon
is worth far more to society than we can well
reckon up. And if, as a result of last Thursday's
events, those just entering upon life, and we all,
shall be warned of the evil and curse of transgression, and be reminded of the surpassing beauty of
honor and faithfulness, and in addition shall catch
an enthusiasm of integrity, it will go no small

way to compensate for the terrible shock that came to this city, and for the agony that has fallen upon so many hearts. . . . We know today that public and private worth are still extant, and that the old cardinal virtues are still held in honor. We need no lantern to find a man."

In the afternoon President Strong, assisted by other clergymen, conducted the funeral service proper at Mr. Heywood's late residence, and paid an equally cordial testimony to the character of the man and to the high quality of heroism which he had displayed. Dr. Strong was able to speak from the point of view of personal friendship and from that of official relation, having been Mr. Heywood's pastor at Faribault in former years, and having been more recently associated with him in connection with the College. It was in a casual conversation which they had held but a few days before the tragedy that Mr. Heywood dropped the remark which showed that he had already decided how he would meet such an ordeal if it ever came to him. The President had been inspecting the new time lock which had just been placed upon the door of the vault. The circumstance recalled to his mind the famous St. Albans bank-raid, which had especially interested him through his personal acquaintance with the victimized cashier. Having spoken of the course pursued by the raiders in that case, he said, in mere playfulness, to Mr. Heywood, "Now if robbers should come in here and order you to open this vault, would you do it?" With a quiet smile, and in his own modest way, Mr. Heywood answered, "I think not." Neither of them dreamed how soon and with what tragical emphasis he would be called to test that resolution.

Mr. Heywood was buried in the Northfield cemetery, at the southern extremity of the city, where his remains still rest and where an unpretentious monument marks his grave.

In an obscure corner of the same cemetery, at night, with neither mourner nor funeral rites, two boxes were buried, supposed to contain the bodies of the dead robbers. No one took the trouble to ascertain the genuineness of the proceeding, or to guard the grave from desecration. That the bodies of criminals belong to anatomical science, is a prevalent opinion. That these criminals were not too good for such a purpose, was readily conceded. That they somehow found their way to a certain medical college, and that one of them was subsequently rescued from its fate by friends, are said to be facts of history.

Northfield, c. 1876, looking east into Bridge Square. The north front of the Scriver Block faces the square; the Dampier Hotel, from which Henry Wheeler directed his devastating fire, can be seen beyond the bridge. (Minnesota Historical Society)

The Scriver Block. The First National Bank (dark sign above
the three window arches, center of photo) lies at the southeast
corner of the Block. (Minnesota Historical Society)

Jesse James, c. 1875
(State Historical Society of Missouri)

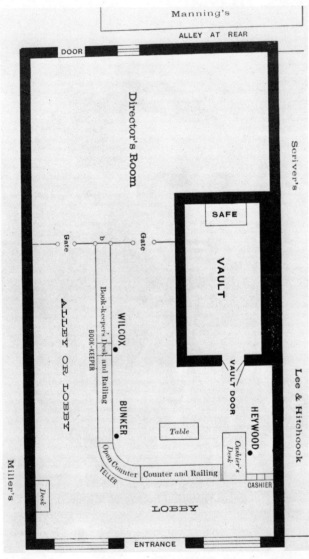

Interior diagram of the First National Bank, showing the locations of its employees at the start of the attempted robbery

Restored bank interior, 1985

Alonzo E. Bunker, the
teller who was wounded
while dashing out the door
at the rear of the bank

Frank J. Wilcox, assistant
bookkeeper of the First
National Bank

Anselm R. Manning, the hardware merchant whose cool aim killed Bill Stiles and wounded Cole Younger

Henry M. Wheeler, the medical student whose fire killed raider Clel Miller and wounded Bob Younger

Action in the street. Woodcut from John Jay Lemon, *The Northfield Tragedy* (1876)

Route of the James-Younger gang, from map owned by the Northfield Historical Society

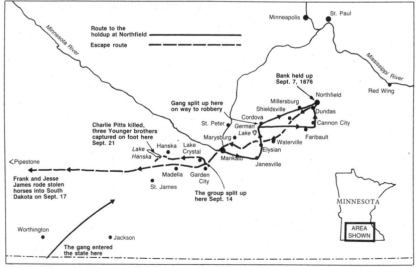

Route to the
holdup at Northfield
Escape route

Minneapolis   St. Paul

Minnesota River

Mississippi River

Red Wing

Bank held up
Sept. 7, 1876

Northfield

Millersburg

Gang split up here
on way to robbery

Shieldsville   Dundas

Cordova   Cannon City

St. Peter

Charlie Pitts killed,
three Younger brothers
captured on foot here
Sept. 21

Marysburg   German
                    Lake   Faribault

Waterville

Hanska   Lake
Lake   Crystal   Elysian
Hanska   Mankato

Pipestone   Janesville

Madelia   Garden
            City

Frank and Jesse
James rode stolen
horses into South
Dakota on Sept. 17

St. James

The group split up
here Sept. 14

Worthington   Jackson

The gang entered
the state here

MINNESOTA

AREA
SHOWN

Jacoby Photo
Minneapolis

The victorious Madelia captors. From left to right: Sheriff
James Glispin, Capt. W. W. Murphy, George Bradford, Ben
Rice, T. L. Vought, Charles Pomeroy, and Jim Severson.
(Minnesota Historical Society)

Heroes and Victims. Clockwise from top: Joseph Lee Heywood, Sheriff James Glispin, Bob Younger, Charley Pitts, Jim
Younger, Cole Younger, and "August Suborn" (pseudonym of
Asle Oscar Sorbel). Bill Chadwell (pseudonym of Bill Stiles)
and Clel Miller occupy center space. The bodies of Pitts,
Chadwell/Stiles, and Miller were photographed after the raid
by Ira E. Sumner of Northfield, although this particular
grouping of photographs was assembled and sold by Minneapolis photographer William H. Jacoby. (Minnesota Historical Society)

Marker, c. 1930, showing location at Hanska Slough of the shoot-out and capture of the Younger brothers (Minnesota Historical Society)

Cole Younger's handwritten response when questioned in Faribault about the identity of Joseph Heywood's murderer (Minnesota Historical Society: original in Northfield Historical Society)

Be true to your friends If the Heavens fall
Cole. Younger.

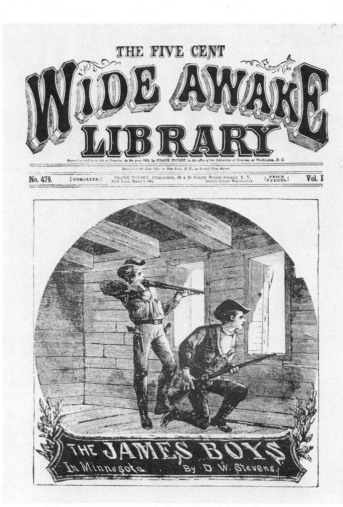

Cover of *The James Boys in Minnesota* (1882), one of the early dime novels penned by the prolific "D. W. Stevens" (pseudonym of John R. Musick) (Minnesota Historical Society)

Bob, Jim, and Cole Younger with their sister Henrietta, photographed at Stillwater State Prison in 1889, two weeks before
Bob Younger's death (Minnesota Historical Society)

Frank James, 1898, four years before he and Cole Younger were reunited (State Historical Society of Missouri)

George Huntington, author of *Robber and Hero*, c. 1889 (Rice
County Historical Society)

W. C. Bronaugh, the Missourian who led efforts to pardon the
Younger brothers. From W. C. Bronaugh, *The Younger's Fight
for Freedom* (1906)

"Jesse James Days" in Northfield, 1948. The re-enactment took place in front of the Jesse James Cafe, around the corner from the old bank (Defeat of Jesse James Committee)

"Defeat of Jesse James Days," 1985

Rendezvous before the raid, 1985 "Defeat of Jesse James Days"

The walk to the bank, 1985 "Defeat of Jesse James Days"

IN

GRATEFUL MEMORY

OF

Joseph Lee Heywood

Formerly

Treasurer of this College.

Born August 12, 1837.

A man modest, true and gentle; diligent in business; conscientious in duty; a citizen benevolent and honorable; towards God reverent and loyal; who, while defending his trust as a bank officer, fearlessly met death at the hands of armed robbers, in Northfield, Sept. 7, 1876.

❧❧❧❧❧

This tablet is inscribed by his friends as a tribute to heroic fiidelty.

ESTO FIDELIS USQUE AD MORTEM.

Inscription of the Carleton College memorial plaque

CHAPTER VI.

PURSUING THE FUGITIVES.

While the excitement over the tragedy was at its height, and the inquests and the funeral services over the dead were in progress, the escaped robbers were not forgotten.

They had left Northfield by what is known as the Dundas Road, leading to the town of that name, three miles to the south. Their original plan had been to go westward, over the route by which they had come, and to stop at the telegraph office on their way, and destroy the instruments, in order that the news of the raid might not be spread till they were out of reach in the great forest tract lying in that direction. But, as they afterwards said, finding it "too hot" for them in that part of the town, they were glad to escape by any route they could find; while the telegraph was publishing their deeds and their descriptions in every direction.

Dundas being the nearest place at which they

could cross the Cannon River, they made all
possible speed toward it,—six men on five horses.
They rode abreast, like a squad of cavalry, taking
the whole road, and compelling every one they
met to take the ditch. Meeting a farmer with a
good span of horses, they stopped him and helped
themselves to one of the horses, for the use of Bob
Younger, who had been riding behind his brother
Cole. A little farther on they "borrowed" a
saddle for him of another farmer, representing
themselves to be officers of the law in pursuit of
horse thieves,—a pretense which they made much
use of during their flight. As soon as possible
they got back into their former route, where they
were once more on somewhat familiar ground.
The death of Miller had deprived them of the
guide upon whose knowledge of the country they
had depended. The loss of their trained and
high-bred saddle-horses was perhaps a still more
serious calamity,—a loss which they were not
able to make good with any of the farm-horses
stolen one after another. Their rush at full speed
through Dundas caused a sensation; but, owing
to the absence of the telegraph operator, the news
of the raid had not been received, and they were
not molested. Millersburg, where some of them
had spent the previous night, was reached about

half-past four. They were recognized by the landlord who had entertained them, but they were still in advance of the news of their crime and far in advance of their pursuers. They rode hard, sparing neither themselves nor their beasts, although Bob Younger's arm was causing him much suffering. His horse fell under him, breaking the saddle-girth, and was abandoned in disgust, Younger again mounting behind one of his companions. Another horse was seized in a similar manner, regardless of the protests of his owner; but the animal balked so obstinately that he too had to be abandoned Thus began a dreary two-weeks flight, which grew more and more dismal day by day, as the fugitives skulked from place to place, now riding, now walking, now hiding, in a region where, as they too well knew, every man's hand was against them. Nature and Providence seemed to be against them, too. A cold, drizzling rain set in the day after the raid, and continued almost incessantly for two weeks. The way of the transgressor was hard, and it grew harder at every step.

The pursuers were after them. Before the robber-cavalcade was out of sight of the scene of their raid, almost before the smoke of the battle had passed away, men were running for

their guns and horses, to join in the chase. The
first movements were made under intense excitement, and were necessarily irresponsible and futile.
But more deliberate measures were soon taken.
Mr. J. T. Ames called for volunteers for a systematic pursuit, and telegraphed to the state capital
for aid. Sheriffs, detectives, chiefs of police and
scores of private citizens promptly responded. As
soon as practicable a small army of pursuers
was organized, and systematic plans for their
transportation and sustenance were perfected.

Three times on Thursday afternoon advanced
detachments of this force encountered the fugitives. First a couple of volunteer scouts,
mounted, by a singular coincidence, on the horses
of the dead robbers, came within sight of the band
as they were seizing the farmer's horse on the
Dundas Road. But as the robbers were six to
the scouts' two, the latter did not venture an
attack, but contented themselves with trailing
their game until reinforcements should arrive.
Again, at Shieldsville, fifteen miles west of Northfield, a squad of Faribault men had arrived in
advance of the pursued by taking a shorter road.
But not knowing how close at hand the bandits
were, they had gone within doors, leaving their
guns outside, when the raiders suddenly appeared

before the door, from which they did not permit their unarmed pursuers to issue, but coolly watered their horses at an adjacent pump, shot a defiant volley of bullets into it, and went on their way. The out-witted scouts quickly regained their guns, and being reinforced by a dozen or more local recruits, hastened after the robbers. The band was overtaken in a ravine about four miles west of Shieldsville, where the two forces exchanged some long-range shots, without effect on either side; and the robbers escaped into the thick woods beyond.

While these preliminary contests were taking place, the more systematic campaign was arranged and inaugurated. Before Thursday night two hundred men were in the field, and on Friday five hundred. Other hundreds still joined the chase later on, swelling the number at one time to at least a thousand. It is impossible to give a list of those engaged, or to do justice to the zeal, the determination and the endurance that they showed. Among those who were prominently engaged, either in organizing the forces or in conducting operations in the field, may be mentioned Mayor Solomon P. Stewart of Northfield, Sheriff Ara Barton and Geo. N. Baxter, Esq., of Faribault, chiefs of police King of St. Paul and Munger of Minneapolis, detectives Hoy and Brissette, and many others. Of the men under them, several were experienced officers, and not a few were veteran soldiers. There were also, of course, in so large and hastily-mustered a force, very many who had no fitness for the service, either in personal qualities or in equipment, and no conception of the requirements of such a campaign. They came armed with small pistols and old fowling-pieces of various degrees of uselessness, and utterly without either judgment or courage. Their presence was a source of weakness to the force. Their foolish indiscretions embarrassed and defeated the best-laid plans; and their failure at critical moments and places to do what they had been depended upon to do made them worse than useless,—worse than enemies. Many went into the service from mercenary motives. Large rewards for the capture of the robbers dead or alive were offered by the Northfield bank, the Governor of the state and the railway companies; and this inducement drew into the ranks of the pursuers much poor material. These statements need to be made, not so much by way of censure upon the inefficient as in justice to the better members of the force, and as an explanation of some of the vexatious delays and failures of the campaign. For, while it constantly suffered from the presence of these mercenaries and blunderers, it did not lack, from its first day to its last, a nucleus of brave, keen-witted, cool-headed, determined men, whom nothing could daunt or discourage.

And the best of them were not too capable for the work. Two objects were to be accomplished, —the retreat of the fugitives was to be cut off, and they were to be hunted down and captured. To secure the first, picket-lines were thrown out in advance of them, covering every route which they could possibly take, and especially guarding roads, bridges and fords. To secure the second, scouting parties were put upon their trail, to follow them from place to place, and to explore the country far and near in search of them. It was no holiday excursion. They were in a vast forest tract known as the Big Woods, broken here and there by clearings and by settlements great and small, but embracing also wide areas of uncut timber, full of dense thickets and ravines, and abounding in lakes, streams and swamps. The weather made difficult trailing, as tracks and other signs were soon obliterated; and the nature and extent of the ground to be covered rendered it impossible to keep the picket-line strong at all points. The rain and the mud, the dripping forests, the swollen streams, the softened fields, multiplied the hardships of the pursuers. Their very numbers caused confusion. They were for the most part unable to recognize with any certainty either the robbers or one another or to tell whether some squad of horsemen in the distance were friends or foes. The bandits were shrewd enough to take advantage of this doubt. It was their favorite trick to pass themselves off as a sheriff's posse in pursuit of the bank-robbers. Under this subterfuge they inquired their way of unsuspecting people, obtained provisions, secured information about the position and movements of their pursuers, and repeatedly supplied themselves with fresh horses. But this is in advance of our story.

We left the robbers in their Thursday night's hiding-place in the woods beyond Shieldsville. Thence on Friday they moved first westward and then southwestward, in the direction of Waterville. Coming to a ford of the Little Cannon River, guarded by three men poorly armed, they were fired upon and turned back into the woods. Finding shortly afterward that the guard had withdrawn, they returned to the ford, crossed over, and disappeared in the forest beyond. Thus the picket line which had been so laboriously posted was broken at its weakest point.

The news of the escape was immediately carried to those in command, a new picket-line was thrown out in advance of the robbers, and the pursuers pressed the more eagerly after them. The whole region was now aroused. The telegraph was kept constantly busy, flashing items of fact, and a good many items of fiction, to and from the field of operations. The railways did good service in transporting men to accessible points; but the flight and the pursuit were chiefly out of the range of towns, telegraphs or railways, in the heart of the forest.

Pushing on into the township of Elysian, the robbers found themselves in a labyrinth of lakes and swamps, where it seemed easy to prevent their escape. At an isolated farm they exchanged two of their exhausted horses for fresh ones, against the owner's protest. In the evening they made a similar exchange in an out-of-the-way pasture without consulting the owner. Late Friday night they went into camp between Elysian and German Lake. The stolen horses were now turned loose, and all returned to their masters. The remaining horses were tied to trees; a sort of tent was made by spreading blankets over some bushes; and under this the fugitives spent the rainy night.

On Saturday morning they abandoned their horses altogether, tied their blankets about their bodies with the bridles, and, though already lame and disabled, continued their journey on foot. The horses were found three days later, one of them still tied to the tree, the other two having gnawed off their halters and escaped. The robbers now proceeded more circumspectly. The dash and daring of their previous course were exchanged for the stealth and caution more befitting their condition. They went no farther on Saturday than to find a hiding-place on an island in the middle of the swamp, where they encamped for the day. After dark they took up their journey, marched slowly all night, and at daylight on Sunday morning again halted, near the village of Marysburg, whose church-bell they could hear from their camp in the woods. Passing around Marysburg, they next encamped four miles south of that village, so slow was their progress and so short their marches. Nine miles west of this camp, and within two or three miles of Mankato, they found a deserted farm-house in the woods, where they spent Monday night, Tuesday and Tuesday night, having advanced less than fifty miles in five days.

Even at this rate they had distanced their pursuers, who did not suspect that they had abandoned their horses, and who, confident that no mounted cavalcade had passed their lines, were still searching the swamps and bottoms about Elysian. This delusion was painfully dispelled on Tuesday morning by the discovery of the half-starved horses and the deserted camp. The robbers had stolen away on foot, and had at least a three-days start. This was regarded as evidence of the hopelessness of the chase. The fugitives were no doubt far away, and in what direction no one could conjecture. A large proportion of the pursuers, including many of the most efficient leaders, therefore gave up the hunt and returned to their homes. Even some authentic reports from persons who had caught glimpses of the robbers near Mankato were scouted as absurdly incredible.

Soon, however, further news was received which could not be disputed, and which at once aroused fresh interest in the chase. On Tuesday the robbers, it seemed, had invited themselves to breakfast at the house of a German farmer. On Wednesday morning they had captured another farmer's hired man in the woods, and after binding him, extorting information from him, threatening to kill him, and finally swearing him to secrecy, had let him go. Believing that a bad promise was better broken than kept, he had immediately reported the incident to his employer, who hastened with the news to Mankato, whence the telegraph sent it everywhere. Excitement was at once renewed. The disbanded forces hurried back, and hundreds of fresh recruits joined in the chase. A thousand men were soon on the ground, and a new campaign was organized under the direction of Gen. Pope of Mankato. Again patrols and searching parties were sent out, and every possible avenue of escape was guarded night and day.

But again the fugitives escaped, not so much by virtue of their own cunning as through favorable accidents and the inefficiency of the guards on duty. Part of them crossed the railroad bridge over the Blue Earth River during Wednesday night. Two others, mounted on a stolen horse, passed the picket-line near Lake Crystal on Thursday night. These last were challenged, fired upon, and probably wounded by a brave young fellow, named Richard Roberts, whose sleeping companions had left him to hold the pass alone. The horse threw his riders and ran away, and they escaped in the darkness to the adjacent field, one of them leaving his hat behind him.

The band had now divided, Pitts and the three Youngers forming one division, and the two Jameses the other. It is believed to have been the James brothers whom Roberts fired upon. Continuing their flight, they stole a fine span of greys, on which they mounted bareback. This capture was a most fortunate one for them, and enabled them to make rapid progress and to assume again the role of officers in pursuit of criminals. They had no difficulty in getting food and information from unsuspecting people, who found only too late how they had been imposed upon. The two men went almost due west during the next forty-eight hours, travelling day and night at the utmost practicable speed, and making eighty miles with scarcely a halt. On Sunday, September 17th, they crossed the Minnesota line into what is now South Dakota. That evening they took the liberty of exchanging their over-driven greys for a span of blacks, one of which proved to be blind in one eye and the other in both. Not finding these satisfactory, they exchanged them in turn, in the small hours of Monday morning, for another span of greys. They now turned southward; passed through Sioux Falls; exchanged salutations with the driver of the Yankton stage, and clothes with a Sioux City doctor; and quietly pursued their flight by a route and to a destination best known to themselves.

They had not been permitted to make this escape without interference. No sooner was it known that they had gone through the picket-line than scouts were sent out in every direction, to over-take or intercept them. The best men in the field took up the trail. The most comprehensive meas-ures were adopted for their capture. But owing perhaps to the unexpected celerity of their move-ments, so different from the previous methods of the gang, and to unforeseen slips and miscalcula-tions, they succeeded in eluding their pursuers, most of whom abandoned the chase at the Dakota line.

This episode had entirely diverted attention from the rest of the band, as it was not then known that a division had taken place; and when the two horsemen were finally lost track of, the general supposition was that the whole band had escaped. Some persons, indeed, believed that the four unaccounted for were still in the neighborhood in which they had last been seen. The disreputa-ble house near Mankato, already referred to as the place where two of the robbers were known to have been on the night of September 3d, was searched, and many suspicious characters in various places were arrested and investigated. This vigilance resulted in securing some criminals, including two notorious horse-thieves, but it discovered no clue to the bank-robbers.

The mortification of the pursuers was intense; and the denunciations heaped upon some of them and the ridicule upon all was a bitter reward for their two weeks of hard service. The failure of their campaign could not be denied. The only consolation they had was in reflecting that they had done their best, and in joining in the general laugh at their own expense. The robber hunt was the great joke of the season.

CHAPTER VII.

A FAMOUS VICTORY.

Thursdays were notable days in the robber-calendar. On Thursday, September 7th, the attack upon the bank was made. On Thursday, the 14th, the trail of the main band was found and lost in the Minnesota valley beyond Mankato; and on the evening of that day the two horsemen went off on their tangent, drawing almost the entire force of the pursuers after them. On Thursday, the 21st, the public was again electrified by the news that the remaining four, who had also been supposed to have escaped, were yet in the state and had been located in the neighborhood of Madelia.

Madelia is a small village in Watonwan County, and on the Watonwan River, about 24 miles southwest of Mankato. One of the principal features of the surrounding country is a chain of picturesque lakes lying a few miles north of the town; while about five miles southwest of the lakes ran the north fork of the Watonwan River, destined to be as famous in the closing scenes of the raid as the Cannon had been at its beginning.

Madelia was one of the towns visited by the robbers in their preliminary survey. About two weeks before the robbery, Cole Younger and one other of the band spent a Sunday at the Flanders House in that place. They asked many questions of the landlord, Col. Vought, and excited some curiosity in the community. Younger expressed his admiration of the adjacent lake region, with whose geography he seemed to have made himself familiar. When the bank-raid occurred, a few days later, Col. Vought immediately understood who his guests had been, and did not doubt that Younger's interest in the topography of the neighborhood had reference to a line of retreat. And when guards were being placed throughout the region to intercept the robbers in their flight, Col. Vought advised guarding a certain bridge between two of these lakes, at a point of which Younger had made special mention, and by which any one acquainted with the region would be sure to pass. This counsel was followed, and Col. Vought himself, with two others, guarded the bridge for two nights.

A few rods from this bridge lived a Norwegian

farmer named Suborn, with his wife and his son Oscar, an intelligent and active lad about seventeen years of age. As the men kept watch at the bridge in the evenings, Oscar would come down and sit with them, talking of the robbers and the robbery, and forming in his mind a pretty distinct idea of the appearance and the tactics of the outlaws. He repeatedly expressed the wish that he might meet them and have a shot at them with his father's old gun. When the band was supposed to have escaped, and the guards were withdrawn, Col. Vought charged Oscar to keep a sharp lookout, and if he saw any fellows that he thought might be the robbers, to come into Madelia and tell the Colonel. This the boy promised to do.

On the morning of September 21st, while Oscar and his father were milking the cows, two men walked by, bidding Oscar a civil good morning as they passed. Something in their appearance instantly convinced the boy that they were the bandits; and he ran to his father and said, "There goes the robbers." His father scouted the idea, and bade him go on with his milking. But the conviction grew upon the boy as he milked, and he soon set down his pail and ran to look after the men, making inquiries of the neighbors and freely expressing his views concerning them.

When he returned to the house, he learned that the men he had seen and two others had been there asking for food, and saying that they were fishermen. Oscar insisted that they were the robbers, and after many objections on his father's part, finally got permission to take a horse and go and tell people what he had seen.

He instantly started for Madelia, seven or eight miles away, urging the old farmhorse to the top of his speed, and shouting to every body he passed "Look out! The robbers are about!" but finding nobody to believe him. A short distance from Madelia the horse fell down, throwing the excited rider into the mud; but he was soon up and away again faster than ever.

Entering Madelia, he rode straight to the Flanders House, according to his promise to Col. Vought. The latter was standing on the porch of the hotel when the messenger dashed up, boy and horse equally out of breath and both of them covered with mud. A few questions sufficed to convince the Colonel that the boy knew what he was talking about, and he immediately siezed his gun, mounted his horse, and started for the Suborn farm. Sheriff Glispin had come up during the conversation with Oscar, and also joined in the chase. Dr. Overholt, W. R. Estes and S. J.

Severson did the same. These five went in company. C. A. Pomeroy heard the news and hastened after them. G. A. Bradford and Capt. W. W. Murphy followed hard, and reached the field in time for effective service. From St. James, a neighboring town, to which the telegraph had carried the news, came G. S. Thompson and B. M. Rice, most of their neighbors being too incredulous or too indifferent to join them. In the immediate vicinity of the robbers all was excitement, and people were gathering in greater and greater numbers as the facts became known.

The first detachment from Madelia had no difficulty in learning where the robbers were, and lost no time in reaching the locality. The band was soon descried, making its way on foot through what is known as Hanska Slough. Sheriff Glispin called upon them to halt; and as they paid no attention to his demand, he and his men fired upon them.

The robbers ran until they were out of sight behind a knoll, and before their pursuers came up with them had crossed Lake Hanska, a considerable body of water. The Madelia men, finding some difficulty in getting their horses through the water, separated, part of them going up stream and part down, in search of crossings. Reaching

the other side, Col. Vought and Dr. Overholt
again caught sight of the robbers, and the Doctor
fired at them, with so good an aim as to hit the
stick with which Cole Younger was walking.
Sheriff Glispin and his two companions now
came up from the other direction. Seeing that the
robbers were making for a herd of horses on an
adjacent farm, the Madelia men intercepted the
movement, and for their pains received a volley
from the enemy's revolvers, the bullets flying thick
about the heads of the pursuers, though at pretty
long range, and one of them grazing Glispin's
horse.

Thus foiled, the bandits went down to the
river-bank, opposite the house of Andrew Anderson, and telling him that they were in pursuit of
the bank-robbers, ordered him to bring his horses
over to them. The old ruse did not work. Instead of putting his horses at the service of the
band, the shrewd farmer ran them off in the
opposite direction. Foiled again, the men went
up the river to a ford, crossed over, and came
down through the Anderson farm to a granary,
where they seemed about to make a stand; but
changing their plan, they made one more effort to
supply themselves with horses. Mr. Horace
Thompson and his son, of St. Paul, were hunting

in the neighborhood, and had two livery teams belonging to Col. Vought, of Madelia. Spying these horses, the robbers made a rush for them. But the Thompsons promptly exchanged their light charges for wire cartridges loaded with goose shot, and prepared to give the free-booters a warm reception. The free-booters did not care to risk the encounter, and turning back, took refuge in the brush in the river-bottom. Mr. Thompson proposed to some of those present to go in after them and hunt them out; but the armed force then present was not thought to be strong enough for such a movement.

The robbers were now hemmed in upon all sides. On the south was a high bluff, curving slightly outward to enclose the low bottom-land at its base. On the north was the Watonwan River, washing the bluff on the left, then swinging away from it in a double curve, and then back toward the bluff again. A rude triangle was thus enclosed, some five acres in extent, nearly level, open in some places, but for the most part covered with an almost impenetrable growth of willows, box-elders, wild plums and grapevines.

The robbers having been driven to cover in these thickets, the next effort was to prevent their escape. A considerable number of people had by

this time collected, some on one side of the river
and some on the other. Glispin and Vought went
down to the lower end of the ravine and posted
guards on the bluffs to watch that point. Meantime Capt. Murphy had arrived, and at once took
similar precautions on the other side of the river.
But they had no intention of waiting for the
robbers to come out, or to give them a chance to
escape, as they had so often done, under cover of
darkness. Capt. Murphy, having made his picket-
line secure on the north side of the river, came
around to the south side, where some of his
Madelia neighbors and other resolute men were
gathered, and proposed that they go into the
brush and rout out the bandits. A number seemed
willing to join him in this attempt; but the list
was much reduced when they heard his startling
instructions as to the method of procedure.
Moreover some of the best men on the ground
had been assigned to guard duty, and were not
available for this service. In a few minutes, however, six brave fellows stood by his side, ready to
go wherever he would lead them.

The roll of this Spartan band of seven is as
follows: Capt. W. W. Murphy, Sheriff James Glispin, Col. T. L. Vought, B. M. Rice, G. A. Bradford,
C. A. Pomeroy, S. J. Severson.

Capt. Murphy formed his men in line, four paces

apart, ordering them to advance rapidly but in line, to keep their arms ready, observe the front well, and the instant the bandits were discovered concentrate the fire of the whole line upon them.

They advanced promptly across the eastern side of the triangle, from the bluff to the river, and then, turning to the left, followed the river's course, with the line at right angles with it. They had advanced some fifty or sixty yards in this direction, when they discovered the robbers, crouching and almost concealed in a thicket of vine-covered willows and plumtrees. At the same instant one of the robbers fired. It was the signal for a general fusilade on both sides. Firing was rapid and at close range, the two forces being not more than thirty feet apart at the center of the line, and all heavily armed. The battle was sharp but brief. Again, as in the Northfield fight, the palm of marksmanship was with the citizens and not with the professional crack-shots. Mr. Bradford had his wrist grazed by a ball as he raised his rifle for his first shot. Another ball grazed Mr. Severson. Another still struck Capt. Murphy in the side, and glancing on a brier-root pipe in his pocket, lodged in his pistol-belt. With these exceptions not a man in the party was touched. Of the robbers, on the other hand, Bob Younger was wounded in the breast; his brother James had five wounds;

Cole had eleven, and Pitts was dead, having been
hit five times. When Capt. Murphy ordered firing
to cease, and called upon the robbers to surrender,
Bob Younger was the only one who could respond. "I surrender," said he, "They are all
down but me." As he rose to his feet at the command of his captors, the movement was not
understood by the guards on the bluff, and they
fired at him, wounding him slightly; but Capt.
Murphy immediately checked the untimely attack.

The arms of the robbers were taken from them,
and they were placed in a wagon and taken to
Madelia in the custody of the sheriff, escorted by
their captors as body-guard, and by a miscellane-
ous company of those who had been directly or
indirectly connected with the engagement. A
mile from town they met another company of
people who had come by special train from other
towns where the news of the reappearance of the
robbers had been received. The visitors found
themselves too late to take part in the capture,
the honor of which belonged solely to local
heroes; but they could join in the general rejoicing
and help to swell the triumphal procession. As
the returning throng entered Madelia, it was
received with great demonstrations of joy, to
which the wounded bandits responded by waving
their hats.

CHAPTER VIII.

THE END OF A BAD ENTERPRISE.

The chagrin and exasperation which followed the escape of the two Jameses were changed to exultation over the victory in the Watonwan bottom,—a victory well worthy to close the campaign so bravely begun in the streets of Northfield. Whatever blunders had been made, whatever hardships and disappointments had been endured, the final result was fairly satisfactory. Of the eight desperados who rode forth so confidently on their career of plunder, three were dead, three were prisoners, and the other two were in ignominious retreat—one of them wounded. They had wasted a month in fruitless effort, lost their splendid horses and equipment, spent much money and gained none, suffered unutterable hardships, and achieved nothing but two brutal and profitless murders.

Arrived in Madelia, the captured men were taken to the Flanders House, where Cole Younger and his now dead comrade Pitts, had played the role of gentlemen travelers a month before. Younger had recognized Col. Vought and saluted him as "landlord" when they met as captor and captive on the bloody field of the Watonwan. He also recognized Mr. G. S. Thompson, who was doing guard duty at the time of the capture, and reminded him of a visit which Pitts and himself had made to Thompson's store in St. James during the same preliminary tour.

The Flanders House was made for the time being a hospital and a prison. Guards were posted within and without, and every precaution was taken to prevent either the escape of the prisoners or any unlawful attack upon them. The men were wet, weakened by fatigue and exposure, nearly famished and shockingly wounded. They received such attention as humanity dictated. Their wounds were dressed; their wet garments were exchanged for dry ones; their hunger was appeased and they were placed in comfortable beds.

They appreciated this treatment most gratefully. They had hardly expected less than being lynched or torn in pieces by the infuriated people; and they repeatedly expressed their admiration both of the bravery of their captors and of the

magnanimity of those who had them so abso-
lutely at their mercy. It was indeed rumored
that a train-load of lynchers was on the way,
bent on summary vengeance; but the officers of
the law and the people of Madelia were prepared
to resist such an attempt to the utmost, and it
never was made.

Sight-seers and lion-hunters came by hundreds,
from every direction. On the day following the
capture the hotel was besieged by an eager throng,
that filled its halls and corridors and the adjacent
street, and kept a continuous stream of visitors
filing through the rooms where the robbers were
confined. Reporters, photographers and detectives were there, each intent on his own professional ends; and every type of sentiment was
represented, from open vindictiveness to morbid
sympathy and admiration for criminal audacity.

The prisoners talked freely on certain subjects,
and with shrewd reserve upon others. They
claimed to be the victims of circumstances, rather
than of their own inclinations. They talked
pathetically of their family and their antecedents,
advised young men to shun bad ways, and re-
quested the prayers of pious women. Being
allowed an opportunity to confer together, they
agreed to admit their own identity, but refused to

divulge that of their companions, either the dead
or the living. They denied that the two who escaped were the James brothers, but would give no
further information concerning them. The work
of identification was effected, however, without
their aid. Chief of Police McDonough, of St.
Louis, and other officers and citizens, were able of
their own knowledge, with the aid of collateral
testimony and of rogues-gallery pictures, to iden-
tify the two killed at Northfield as Clel Miller and
Bill Stiles, and the one killed in the capture as
Charley Pitts, alias George Wells. Little doubt
was entertained, also, that the ones who escaped
were Jesse and Frank James, who about that time
reappeared in their old haunts in Missouri.

On Saturday, September 23d, the prisoners
were delivered to Sheriff Barton of Rice County,
by whom they were taken to Faribault and safely
lodged in the county jail, a few miles from the
scene of their crime.

Here, again, they were visited by multitudes of
people of all sorts and conditions, and received
many attentions, pleasant and unpleasant, as the
reward of bad notoriety. Here also they were
menaced with a threatened lynching, this time a
dead-in-earnest affair, prevented only by the vigilance and determination of the officers of the law,

aided by the citizens of Faribault. So strongly
was the jail guarded, and so strict was the
discipline maintained in its defence, that when a
member of the city police one night approached
the guard, making some motion that was deemed
suspicious, and imprudently neglecting to respond
to the challenge of the guard, he was fired upon
and killed.

The 9th of November, just nine weeks after the
attack upon the Northfield bank, was another
fateful Thursday in the robber-calendar. On that
day they were arraigned for trial before the Rice
County District Court, at Faribault, Judge
Samuel Lord presiding, and G. N. Baxter, Esq.,
being the prosecuting officer. On the previous
day the sister and the aunt of the three prisoners
had arrived, to attend them during the ordeal.
The refinement and respectability of these ladies
served to emphasize yet more strongly the social
standing from which the men had fallen and the
needlessness of the disgrace which they had
brought upon themselves and their friends.

The arraignment presented one of the most
dramatic scenes in connection with the crime.
The prisoners, in expectation of the summons,
had prepared themselves to make the best possible
appearance in public. The three were shackled

together, Cole in the middle, with Bob on the right and Jim on the left. The sheriff, chief of police and his lieutenant walked by their side, an armed guard marched before them and another behind them. The robbers somewhat distrusted the temper of the crowd that filled the streets; and there were some mutterings of a threatening nature, but no overt acts of hostility. At the court-house the guards opened to the right and left, to admit the sheriff and his prisoners and prevent the entrance of improper persons.

Four indictments had been found against the prisoners by the Grand Jury. The first charged them with being accessory to the murder of Heywood; the second with attacking Bunker with intent to do great bodily harm; the third with robbing the First National Bank of Northfield. The fourth charged Cole Younger as principal, and his brothers as accessories, with the murder of Nicholas Gustavson, the Swede whom the robbers shot for remaining on the street when ordered to leave. These indictments having been read, the prisoners were, at the request of their counsel, allowed two days to decide how they would plead. It was a question of peculiar difficulty. On the one hand, to plead guilty was to renounce all hope of eluding justice through the loopholes of legal technicality. On the other hand, to plead not guilty was to ensure the severest penalty in case of conviction. For the laws of Minnesota were then such that if a murderer pleaded guilty, capital punishment could not be inflicted upon him. This law, designed to prevent long and needless trials in a certain class of cases, afforded these criminals an advantage which the public bitterly begrudged them, but of which, in view of the practical certainty of conviction, they decided to avail themselves.

Accordingly, being again arraigned in court, on the following Saturday, they pleaded guilty to all the indictments. Whereupon Judge Lord pronounced upon them the severest penalty then allowed by the law,—imprisonment for life.

A few days later, Sheriff Barton, with the aid of a strong guard, conducted the robbers to Stillwater; and the State Prison, the goal of so many a criminal career, closed its doors upon them. Though commonly regarded as but the second-best place for them, it has thus far safely held them, except in the case of one of them, whose sentence has expired under the great Statute of Limitation. Robert died in prison, September 16th, 1889. Many attempts have been made to secure pardons for the others; but thus far no governor has been found willing to accede to such a request.

CHAPTER IX.

No extended biographical notices are compatible with either the purpose or the limits of this book; nor is a large amount of such matter desirable. The deeds that have been recounted speak for themselves and the men who performed them. Yet many readers will doubtless desire to know something more of the personality of those men, of their antecedents and their subsequent career. The brief sketches which follow relate solely to those who were actively connected with the three most important scenes in the narrative,—the struggle in the bank, the fight on the street, and the capture of the four robbers near Madelia.

JOSEPH LEE HEYWOOD was born at Fitzwilliam, New Hampshire, August 12, 1837. His parents upon both sides were of the sturdiest New England stock. His father was an energetic and progressive farmer, taking much interest in public affairs, state and national, in politics a Whig, and later a Republican, and an opponent of slavery. His mother was a devout and conscientious woman, unwavering in her moral convictions, and unselfishly devoted to her children. She sought to inspire in them the highest ideas of honor, truth and duty; and they were accustomed to ascribe to her, more than to any other influence, whatever virtues of character they developed.

Our hero's early life was spent on the farm. The rudiments of education acquired at the district school, were supplemented by reading and study at home, until he became well fitted for the practical affairs of life. When about twenty years of age he left home, to make his own way in the world. He spent about a year in Concord, Mass., another in Fitchburg, another in New Baltimore, Michigan, where he was clerk in a drug-store, and then a part of a year in Moline, Illinois, whence he went to Chicago in 1862, the second year of the Civil War.

Reared as he had been, and trained from childhood to the love of truth, country and freedom, his enlistment in the Union army was almost a matter of course. He became a member of the 127th Illinois Regiment in August, 1862, went with his regiment to the front, and at once engaged in active service. Among other movements in which he participated were the siege of Vicksburg and the capture of Arkansas Post. The hardships of army life proved too severe for his constitution, and his health gave way under them, necessitating his removal first to the hospital and then to the home of his brother in Illinois. Recovering sufficiently after a time to permit of his performing light army service, he was detailed as druggist in the Dispensary at Nashville, Tennessee, where he remained until his final discharge from the service at the close of the War, in 1865.

After a year spent mainly with his brother in Illinois, he came to Minnesota, residing first in Faribault, then in Minneapolis, and finally, in the autumn of 1867, removing to Northfield. Here he was for five years employed as a book-keeper in the lumber-yard of Mr. S. P. Stewart. In 1872 he accepted the position of book-keeper in the First National Bank, a position which he filled with fidelity for four years, and in defence of whose trusts he forfeited his life.

Mr. Heywood was twice married; first to Miss Mattie Buffum, and after her death, to Miss Lizzie Adams. Both were natives of Massachusetts, and both were women of superior character. A daughter five years of age, the child of the first wife, survived her father. She has since graduated from Carleton College, and also from the School of Music connected with that institution, and is now (1895) an accomplished teacher of music in her native state.

As has been elsewhere stated, Mr. Heywood's sterling integrity and business ability brought him into many positions of responsibility, among which were those of Treasurer of the City of Northfield and Treasurer of Carleton College. His personal traits have been so well characterized and his place in the estimation of those who knew him so well defined in the funeral address of the Rev. Mr. Leonard, quoted on pages 42 to 45, that further words in that direction are needless. His memory has ever been cherished with peculiar reverence by the people of Northfield, especially by the College of which he was an officer; and his heroic character was admired wherever the story was known. The banks of the United States and Canada contributed a fund of over twelve thousand dollars for the benefit of his family, and as a tribute to his heroism. The Grand Army Post in Northfield is named for him, and his portrait hangs in their hall. The College has a fund of $2,500, called "The Heywood Library Fund,"

founded in his honor; his portrait and a memorial
tablet in commemoration of him hang in the College library; and a memorial window in the First
Congregational Church of Northfield bears his
name and the inscription "FIDELITAS." No
word could better characterize the man and epito-
mize his life.

The following lines, from the New York Tribune,
are the tribute of a well-known poet to Mr. Heywood's heroism:

ON A FAITHFUL BANK CASHIER.

(From the New York Tribune.)

Unto how few the fadeless bays
    Belong! How few the iron crown
Of virtue wear! And few the lays
    That bear a hero's honor down
Untarnished to the latest days!

Yet there was one but now who breathed,
    Faithful to trust, and in that hour
Summoned, he laid down life, bequeathed
    To all good men his good deed's power,
And with great names his name enwreathed.

For tell me not his place was low,
    His sterling voice till then unheard.
He knew and dared to answer "No!"
    Whole volumes spoke in that one word,
And duty could no further go.

Not oftenest on war's glorious field,
        Or in the gaze of favoring men,
Does duty call, but when the shield
        Of secrecy protects, or when
Our dearest hopes to her must yield.

Not oftenest does the martyr gain
        By sacrifice his righteous fame:—
And this man knew it, stood the strain
        Of silent trial. He prized the name
Of truth, and kept it free from stain.

If he betrayed not, death was sure;
        Before him stood the murderous thief.
He did not flinch. . . . Of one life fewer
        The angels turned the blood-sealed leaf
That night, and said: "The page is pure."

O simple faith and loyalty!
        If each true heart like this were strong,
The nation's ancient majesty
        Would rise again with joyous song,
Her beauty shine o'er every sea.

                      GEORGE PARSONS LATHROP.
Cambridge, Mass.

ALONZO E. BUNKER, second son of Enos A.
and Martha M. Bunker, was born at Littleton,
New Hampshire, March 29th, 1849. He came to
Dodge County, Minnesota, in 1855; received a
common-school education in the public schools of
Mantorville; learned the printing business in the
office of the Mantorville Express, and in due time

became the foreman of the office. He taught
school for a short time, after which he entered
the St. Paul Business College, from which he
graduated in 1869. The following year he was
associated with Professor W. W. Payne in the
publication of the Minnesota Teacher, an educational Journal, issued at St. Anthony, now East
Minneapolis. In 1871 he entered the Preparatory
department of Carleton College, where he continued his studies for two years earning the means
of paying his expenses by working at his trade,
teaching and keeping books, until the incessant
application had seriously impaired his health.

In 1873 he entered the service of the First
National Bank of Northfield, in which he continued for about five years. During this period he
served the College as its accountant, and also as
the teacher of book-keeping. He was married, in
1875, to Miss Nettie L. Smith of Red Wing,
Minnesota.

The part taken by Mr. Bunker in the encounter
with the robbers in the bank, as detailed in
Chapter III, shows him to be a man of nerve,
cool and self-collected in danger, and capable of
bold action. Though not subjected to the brutal
treatment inflicted upon Mr. Heywood, he was
subjected to a similar temptation to secure his

own safety by yielding to the demands of the robbers; and he kept such possession of his faculties, mental and physical, as to seize the first opportunity—an opportunity not afforded to Heywood—to break from his captors and escape under fire. The wound which he received at that time was a dangerous one, and narrowly missed being fatal, and the effects of the nervous shock are still felt at times.

In 1878 Mr. Bunker resigned his position in the First National Bank to accept one in the Citizens Bank, of the same city. In 1880 he became connected with the Western Newspaper Union, in which he held responsible positions in Kansas City and St. Paul. In 1882 he went to Helena, Montana, where he assisted in organizing the Second National Bank, of which he was for three years the cashier. His health then requiring a more active life, he engaged for a time in stock-raising and mining operations. In 1888 he returned to the Newspaper Union, of which he is now one of the principal officials, with head-quarters at Chicago.

Mr. Bunker has found time amid his manifold occupations to perform various collateral duties. For a time while in Montana he acted as correspondent of Chicago and St. Paul papers. He has also been active in religious work. While he lived in Helena, he and Mrs. Bunker were largely instrumental in organizing and building up the First Congregational Church of that city.

FRANK J. WILCOX is the son of the late Rev. James F. Wilcox, a clergyman of the Baptist denomination, who held various important positions, pastoral and official, at the East and at the West. Mr. Wilcox was born in Taunton, Mass., September 8th, 1848. Changes in his father's pastorates took him when five years old to Trenton, New Jersey, and when ten years old to Northfield, Minnesota, where he has ever since resided, excepting during the temporary absences of college life.

His education was begun in the public schools. Upon the opening of the Preparatory department of Carleton College, in 1867, he entered the institution, in which he remained until the completion of his preparation for college. His college course was taken in the Chicago University, from which he was graduated in 1874, in the class with President Sutherland of Nebraska, Rev. C. H. D. Fisher, missionary to Japan, and others.

Returning to his Northfield home after his graduation, Mr. Wilcox did not immediately settle down to his vocation in life, but for a time pursued various temporary occupations, one of which was that of assistant in the First National Bank. It was here that he was found by the bank-robbers when they made their raid upon the bank in 1876.

Mr. Wilcox was not subjected to so severe an ordeal as were Heywood and Bunker, as his position gave the robbers less reason to make demands upon him and less excuse for molesting him; but so far as occasion required he co-operated with his colleagues in maintaining the attitude of passive resistance which made the attempted robbery a failure. Immediately after the raid he was appointed to a permanent position in the bank, where he has remained continuously ever since. He is now the Assistant Cashier. He is also prominently connected with other business enterprises in the city, and has held various official positions, educational and municipal. He was married in 1879 to Miss Jennie M. Blake. Both of them are leaders in the social and religious life of the community especially in the Baptist Church of which they are members.

ANSELM R. MANNING was born in Canada, not far from Montreal. By trade he was a carpenter. He was also an adept at blacksmithing, a competent surveyor, and a successful man of business. Possessing this Yankee versatility and knack at turning his hand to almost anything, it was natural that he should seek his home in the United States. He came to Northfield in 1856. Here he pursued his various vocations, mechanical, mathematical and commercial, as occasion seemed to demand. When the railroad was to be constructed through Northfield, he helped to survey it. When the increased facilities which it afforded brought an increase of business, he went into trade, establishing the stove and hardware store so long a familiar feature on Bridge Square.

It was here that he received the visit from a member of the robber band on the morning of the raid, and here that he and his trusty rifle were found ready for the bloody encounter which shortly followed. Mr. Manning is a quiet, good-natured, peaceable man, the last man to seek or desire conflict, but well qualified to meet it when it is forced upon him. He is alert, observant, quick to take the measure of a situation, and prompt and fearless in action.

He still resides in Northfield with his wife and children, and still goes as unobtrusively as ever about his daily business, with no apparent consciousness of being what his neighbors hold him to be, the hero who turned the tide of battle.

HENRY M. WHEELER, the son of Mason and Huldah W. Wheeler, was born in North Newport, New Hampshire, June 23d, 1854. In 1856 the family removed to Northfield, Minnesota, where they arrived on the Fourth of July. Minnesota was still a territory, and Northfield an embryo village, of whose life and development the Wheelers became a part.

Henry began his education in the public school of Northfield; took the preparatory course of study in Carleton College; graduated in medicine from the University of Michigan in 1877, and from the College of Physicians and Surgeons in New York in 1880. He was still a student, at home on a summer vacation, when the robbers made their appearance in Northfield. At the time when they were approaching the bank for the attack, he was sitting as the reader will remember, in front of the drug-store of Wheeler & Blackman, of which his father was one of the proprietors. Regarding the movements of the strangers as suspicious, he followed and watched them, and had already shouted an alarm when he was driven from the street at the point of a pistol. How promptly he secured a weapon, and with what deadly execution he used it, has been duly related. Had the gun been better and the ammunition more

abundant, he would no doubt have given still
more emphatic proof that a doctor may upon occasion make himself more useful in giving wounds
than in healing them. One, at least, of those he
gave that day was so far unprofessional as to
leave no chance for the surgeon's services.

Dr. Wheeler settled in Grand Forks, North
Dakota, in 1881, and still remains there in a large
and successful practice.

JAMES GLISPIN was of Irish descent, but was
born on American soil. He was a man of slight
physical proportions, about five feet, six inches in
height, but possessing great strength, quickness
and endurance, as well as unlimited courage. He
had a magnetic influence over men, and was noted
both for the skill with which he was able to quell
the unruly and the prowess with which when necessary he could overcome larger men than himself
in a trial of strength. After a brief business career,
he was elected Sheriff of Watonwan County. He
proved one of the most popular officers in the
state, and was serving his second term at the time
of the robber-raid. The promptness with which
he started after the bandits on the day of the capture, and the important part taken by him in the
capture itself has been related. It was to his care

also that they were committed after the capture, and upon him rested the responsibility of holding them until they could be turned over to the authorities of the county in which their crimes had been committed.

Mr. Glispin left Madelia in 1880, and went to California, where he engaged in mercantile business. In 1883 he removed to Spokane, Washington, where his fitness for official life was soon recognized. He was elected Sheriff for a two-years term, and was re-elected for two years more. At the close of his second term he went into the real-estate business, in which he continued until his death in 1890.

WILLIAM W. MURPHY was born in Ligonier, Westmoreland County, Pennsylvania, July 27th, 1837. On leaving school in 1854, he went to California, seeking his fortune in the gold-mines. Here he remained till 1861, when he returned to his native state, and took up his residence in Pittsburg. When the call came for volunteers for the Union army, he assisted in raising Company G, of the 14th Pennsylvania Regiment, and entered the service as 2nd Lieutenant of that company. He was promoted to a first lieutenancy, on his merit as an officer; was brevetted Captain by the Secretary of War for gallantry on the field of battle at Piedmont, Va., and was appointed as Captain of Company D in the same regiment, the first vacancy occurring after the brevet.

During the first two years of the war he served in West Virginia, one year under Gen. Sheridan. After Lee's surrender, Capt. Murphy's regiment was ordered to Texas, overland; but when they had reached Leavenworth, Kansas, they received news of the surrender of all the rebel forces in Texas, and the regiment was mustered out at Leavenworth. He received a gunshot wound in the elbow at Lexington, and a sabre wound in the head and another in the arm in a cavalry charge at Piedmont.

In 1866 Capt. Murphy married and settled in Madelia, Minnesota, where he engaged in farming and stock-raising. He has ever been a highly respected and influential citizen, and in 1871 was elected to the Legislature, where he served with credit. He is a man of marked intelligence, especially upon agricultural subjects and is possessed of great coolness and daring. When he came upon the field at the Watonwan, where the robbers were to be routed out of their hiding-place, his assumption of command was accepted as quite a matter of course.

THOMAS LENT VOUGHT was descended on
his father's side from one of the old colonial
Dutch families of New York, and on the side of
his mother from the early pioneers of Orange
County. He was born in Walcott, Wayne
County, April 29th, 1833. His boyhood was
chiefly spent on his father's farm on the shore of
Lake Ontario. He lost his mother by death when
he was seven years old, and his father at seventeen. In the year preceding the father's death
the family had emigrated to Rock county, Wisconsin. At nineteen years of age Thomas went to
La Crosse, where he was employed first as a lum-
berman and afterwards in a hotel, and where, in
1827, he was married to Miss Hester Green. Two
years later the young people settled on a farm at
Bryce Prairie, where they remained until the opening of the War of the Rebellion. Mr. Vought then
enlisted in the 14th Wisconsin Regiment, in which
he served throughout the War.

In 1866 he removed with his family to Madelia,
Minnesota, then so far on the frontier that their
house was the first one in Watonwan County to
be painted and plastered. For the next five years
Mr. Vought operated a line of mail and passenger
stages. When the building of the railroad rendered the stage obsolete, he purchased the

Flanders Hotel, destined to become famous in connection with the two visits—one voluntary and the other involuntary—of the bank robbers in 1876, as already stated.

Since that time, Col. Vought has resided at different times in New York, Dakota and Wisconsin, as health and other interests dictated, and has been now a farmer, now a merchant, now a landlord. His present residence is La Crosse, Wisconsin, where Mrs. Vought died on Nov. 17th, 1894. They have had seven children, of whom four are still living.

BENJAMIN M. RICE was the son of Hon. W. D. Rice, a distinguished citizen of St. James, Minnesota. He was born in Green County, Alabama, February 8th, 1851. In the following year his father removed to Arkansas. Benjamin was educated at the Christian Brothers College in St. Louis. In 1869 the family came to Minnesota, and in 1870 they settled in St. James. The town was not then surveyed. In 1873 he was appointed as engrossing clerk in the state legislature, in which his father repeatedly served as a member.

The young man was noted for both the ardent, impetuous temperament and the chivalrous manners of the southern gentleman. He was excep-

tionally expert in the use of arms, being, it is said,
for quickness and accuracy of aim, the equal of
any of the robbers whom he encountered at the
Watonwan. He was one of the two men from St.
James whom the news of the reappearance of the
robbers drew to the scene, Mr. G. S. Thompson
being the other; and he was one of the coolest
in the contest that followed. A comrade who
marched by his side says that he "seemed to be in
his element."

In the autumn following the capture Mr. Rice
removed to Murfreesboro, Tennesee. Here he was
married soon after to Miss Sallie Bell Wright of
that city. After a few years spent in commercial
business there, he removed to Lake Weir, Florida,
where he died August 14th, 1889, leaving a
widow and two children. Mrs. Rice did not long
survive him, but the son and the daughter still
reside in Florida.

GEORGE A. BRADFORD was born near the
village of Patriot, on the Ohio River in the state
of Indiana, on the 28th of June, 1847. When
about twenty years of age, he emigrated with his
parents to the then new state of Minnesota. For
the next six years he divided his time between
farming and school-keeping, working on the farm

in the summer and teaching school in the winter. In 1873 he became a clerk in a store, and after a time went into business on his own account. He was married in 1877 to Miss Flora J. Cheney, of Madelia. Mr. Bradford is well educated, and much respected in the community in which he lives, and a man of the highest integrity, and of great firmness of character. His modesty is shown in that when responding to the writer's request for biographical material for this notice, he had much more to say about the virtues of his comrades in the fight than about himself.

He was one of the last to arrive at the scene of battle, but one of the first to respond to the call for men to enter the robbers' retreat. He was slightly wounded in the engagement; but the wound did not prevent his doing his full share in the capture of the bandits.

Mr. Bradford has retired from business and is now engaged in farming at Madelia.

CHARLES A. POMEROY was born in Rutledge, Cattaraugus County, New York. His father, Mr. C. M. Pomeroy, was one of the earliest settlers in Madelia, Minnesota, having come to that place in 1855, while Minnesota was still a territory. He became one of the leading citizens of the community, a justice of the peace, etc. The young man was early inured to the hardships and the exigencies of pioneer life,— a good school in which to train one for such emergencies as that with which, as we have seen, he was destined to be identified. He was also a witness of some of the scenes of the great Indian uprising and massacre which swept over that part of Minnesota in 1862.

Mr. Pomeroy is described as short, compact, powerfully built, quiet in disposition, industrious and unobtrusive, yet cool and courageous in danger. He did not hear of the proximity of the robbers on that memorable 21st of September until the first squad of Madelia men had started for the scene; but the moment the news reached his ears, he armed himself, mounted his horse and hastened after them, reaching the field in season to offer himself as one of the seven volunteers who undertook the perilous attack. Mr. Pomeroy was married in 1879, and his home is still in Madelia.

S. J. SEVERSON was born in Wisconsin, in 1855, of Norwegian parents, the only one of that nationality among the seven captors. Coming, in the course of time to Minnesota, he spent several

years on a farm, after which he became a clerk in
a store, where he was employed at the time of the
raid. A published description of him at that time
by one who knew him well, thus characterizes
him: " The jolliest and most popular young man,
especially among his customers. He speaks several
languages well. To his wit and good nature
everybody will bear witness, especially the ladies.
He is a good salesman, industrious, correct and to
be depended on. He is short, stout, and a little
'dare-devil' if any trouble is on hand."

Mr. Severson quickly caught the news of the
discovery of the robbers, and was among the first
to join in the chase and in the attack, shooting at
them in the open ground, following them through
the slough, and hunting them in their hiding-place.
Like Mr. Bradford, he was slightly wounded in
the wrist at the first shot from the robbers,—a
mere graze of the skin, but enough to remind him
that they were not shooting into the air.

Mr. Severson's present home is in Brookings,
South Dakota.

OSCAR OLESON SUBORN was, like Mr. Severson, the son of Norwegian parents, but born on
American soil. Little is known of his life excepting
the events narrated in Chapter VII, in connection

with the capture; every effort of the writer,
seconded by those of obliging friends, having failed
to discover any trace of the brave boy who was
the Paul Revere of the final victory, and whose
name may well close our Roll of Honor.

CHAPTER X.

THE HEYWOOD MEMORIAL FUND.

The following circular and statement concerning the fund contributed by the banks of the United States and Canada, as a testimonial to the heroism of Mr. Heywood, explain themselves:

TO BANKS AND BANKERS.

On the 7th day of September, 1876, Mr. J. L. Heywood, Acting Cashier of the First National Bank of Northfield, Minnesota, was instantly killed by a pistol shot, while refusing to open his safe in obedience to the commands of a gang of ruffians who entered the bank in broad daylight with the avowed intention of robbery. Eight desperadoes, heavily armed (now supposed to be the James and Younger Brothers, of Missouri, and others), rode into town about noon and commenced shooting at all who made their appearance on the streets, while three of their number entered the bank. The citizens quickly comprehended the position, and with such firearms as they could command, opened fire on the horsemen, killing two of their number, and causing the others to take flight. Mr. Heywood could have saved his life by surrendering his trust, but, with a knife actually grazing his throat, replied that they could kill him, but that he would not open the safe.

Does not such a noble devotion to duty, in such marked contrast as it is to the frequent reports of defaulting clerks, demand of the Banking interest of the country some recognition. This young man leaves a widow and one child in dependent circumstances. A voluntary offering on the part of each of the Banks and Bankers of the country, as a recognition of the rare fidelity to duty of Mr. Heywood, would place his family above want, and serve while the memory of this sad affair shall last, to show that faithfulness in places of trust is and will be appreciated.

In view of the above facts, a meeting of the Banks and Bankers of St. Paul, Minnesota, was held on September 19th, at which Five Hundred Dollars was subscribed, and Messrs. H. P. Upham, Jno. S. Prince, and Walter Mann, were appointed a committee to receive contributions for this object, and instructed to issue this circular appeal to the Banks and Bankers of the country.

Your attention is called to the following extract from the Boston Advertiser, which has suggested this action:

THE HERO OF NORTHFIELD.

"The bank cashier, Mr. J. L. Heywood, of
Northfield, Minn., who, with a bowie-knife at his
throat and a pistol at his temple, returned a
decisive "No" to the demand of the gang of
robbers that he should open the bank vault to be
plundered, is rightly enrolled among the heroes of
our times. In him fidelity and courage of the
noblest quality were illustrated again. He is
dead, but the trust committed to him was
not betrayed, and his name will live in honor.
He fell at the post of duty as gallantly as any
knight of any age. He has done the world a
service. We know nothing of his history but this
one act for which he died, but it is enough. He
belonged to the high order of manhood which
yields to no threat, and calmly confronts all the
odds of fate. Whether he has left father or
mother, wife or child, we do not know; but if he
has they have reason to be proud of their relation
to such a man. The whole banking interest of the
country owes him a debt. If he has left any who
were dependent on him, they should be placed
above the possibility of want. The bank he saved
can afford to do this alone, but we hope it will be
done handsomely and promptly by a combined
movement on the part of all the banking institutions of the country. The encouragement of such
conduct is the wisest measure of protection
they can resort to. There ought to be such
a testimonial of appreciation of his unquailing
fidelity as will distinguish the example forever."

H. Thompson, Prest. First National Bank, St. Paul.
D. A. Montfort, Vice-Prest. Second National Bank, St. Paul.
M. Auerbach, Prest. Merchants National Bank, St. Paul.
F. Willius, Prest. German American Bank, St. Paul.
Jno. S. Prince. Prest. Savings Bank, St. Paul.
O. B. Turrell, Prest. Marine Bank, St. Paul.
Jno. Farrington, Prest. Farmers & Mechanics Bank, St. Paul.
Dawson & Co., Bankers, St. Paul.

Please direct your replies to any of the above Banks, and they will be promptly acknowledged and faithfully applied.

St. Paul, Minnesota, Sept. 20, 1876.

THE RESPONSE.

St. Paul, Minn., February 1st, 1877.

To the Subscribers to the "Heywood Fund:"—The undersigned, a committee appointed at a meeting of the Banks and Bankers of St. Paul, Minnesota, Sept. 19th, 1876, to issue a circular appeal to all Banks and Bankers in the United States and Canada, requesting voluntary contributions in aid of the family of JOSEPH LEE HEYWOOD, late Acting Cashier of the First National Bank, of Northfield, Minn., respectfully report that on Sept. 20th, 1876, we prepared a circular, and mailed about seven thousand copies, to all Banks, Bankers, and Savings Banks in the United States, Territories, and Canada.

In response to which we have received in cash........$12,701.57
Less amount paid for printing and postage............. 99.51

$12,602.06
The First National Bank of Northfield donated to
    Mrs. Heywood and the child, direct,..................... 5.000.00

Sum total contributed..$17,602.06
We have paid to Mrs. Joseph Lee Heywood, now
    residing at 627 North Meridian Street, Indian-
    apolis, Ind.,..$ 6,301.03
We have paid to J. C. Nutting, President of the First
    National Bank of Northfield, Guardian of Lizzie
    May Heywood, only child of Joseph Lee Heywood 6,301.03

$12,602.06

It is estimated that upwards of ten thousand dollars has been expended by the First National Bank of Northfield, the State and County authorities, and private citizens, in capturing the robbers.

Of the eight robbers, two were killed on the spot, one was killed and three captured about two weeks after the attempted robbery, and two succeeded in making their escape. Under our defective law concerning capital punishment, the three captured scoundrels saved their necks by pleading guilty to the charge of murder, and are now in the penitentiary for life.

                HENRY P. UPHAM,
                WALTER MANN,
                JOHN S. PRINCE,
                        Committee.

LIST OF CONTRIBUTORS TO THE HEYWOOD FUND.

MINNESOTA.

First National Bank	Northfield.
First National Bank	St. Paul.
Second National Bank	"
Merchants National Bank	"
German American Bank	"
Dawson & Co.	"
Marine Bank	"
Farmers & Mechanics Bank	"
Savings Bank	"
" A Friend "	"
Northwestern National Bank	Minneapolis.
Merchants National Bank	"
First National Bank	"
National Exchange Bank	"
State National Bank	"
Hennepin Co. Sav. Bank	"
Citizens National Bank	Faribault.
C. H. Whipple	"
First National Bank	Kasson.
First National Bank	Shakopee.
First National Bank	Lake City.
A Printer	Waseca.
First National Bank for Customer	Le Roy.
Citizens National Bank	Mankato.
Farmers National Bank	Owatonna.
Bank of Worthington	Worthington.
First National Bank	Stillwater.
Chadbourn Bros. & Co.	Blue Earth City.
Farmers & Traders Bank	Hastings.
O. Roos	Taylors Falls.
First National Bank	Faribault.
Lumbermens National Bank	Stillwater.
H. D. Brown & Co.	Albert Lea.
First National Bank	Red Wing.
Pierce, Simmons & Co.	Red Wing.

First National Bank	Austin.
Bank of Farmington	Farmington.
H. H. Bell	Duluth.
City Bank	Minneapolis.
Eddy & Erskine	Plainview.
First National Bank	St. Peter.
First National Bank	Hastings.

MASSACHUSETTS.

Monson National Bank	Monson.
Merchants National Bank	Salem.
Geo. L. Ames	Salem.
Franklin Co. Natl. Bank	Greenfield.
Adams National Bank	North Adams.
First National Bank	Northampton.
Lechmere National Bank	East Cambridge.
Framingham National Bank	Framingham.
Asiatic National Bank	Salem.
Geo. E. Bullard	Boston.
Salem Savings Bank	Salem.
Safety Fund National Bank	Fitchburg.
Naumkeag National Bank	Salem.
National City Bank	Boston.
C. C. Barry	Boston.
Northboro National Bank	Northboro.
Mercantile National Bank	Salem.
Charles River National Bank	Cambridge.
Bay State National Bank	Lawrence.
Crocker National Bank	Turners Falls.
South Danvers National Bank	Peabody.
Worcester National Bank	Worcester.
City National Bank	"
Central National Bank	"
Merchants National Bank	"
Security National Bank	"
Quinsigamond National Bank	"
Citizens National Bank	"
First National Bank	"

Worcester Co. Inst. for Savings	Worcester.
Worcester Mechanics Savings Bank	"
Peoples Savings Bank	"
Worcester Five Cent Savings Bank	"
Worcester Safe Dep. & Trust Co.	"
Salem National Bank	Salem.
National Granite Bank	Quincy.
Central National Bank	Lynn.
Townsend National Bank	Townsend.
Housatonic National Bank	Stockbridge.
Leicester National Bank	Leicester.
Conway National Bank	Conway.

RECEIVED THROUGH THE ASSOCIATED BANKS OF BOSTON.

Taunton National Bank	Taunton.
Old Boston National Bank	Boston.
Second " "	"
Merchants " "	"
Howard " "	"
Suffolk " "	"
Faneuil Hall " "	"
Blackstone " "	"
Tremont " "	"
Exchange " "	'
Maverick " "	"
Revere " "	"
North " "	"
Shoe & Leather " "	"
Shawmut " "	"
Everett " "	"
Third " "	"
Eagle " "	"
Traders " "	"
First " "	"
Market " "	"
Redemption " "	"
Webster " "	"
Hamilton " "	"

Freemans National Bank	Boston.
Massachusetts " "	"
Boylston " "	"
New England " "	"
Hide & Leather " "	"
Mass. Hosp. Life Ins. Co.	"
Union Safe Dep. Vaults	"
Appleton National Bank	Lowell.
Railroad " "	"
Chapin Banking Co.	Springfield.
Bank of Brighton	Brighton.
Warren National Bank	Peabody.
Millers Rivers National Bank	Athol.
First National Bank	Greenfield.
Cambridge City National Bank	Cambridge.
Pacific National Bank	Nantucket.
Merchants National Bank	Newburyport.
Newburyport Savings Bank	"
First National Bank	"
Ocean National Bank	"
Mechanics National Bank	"
Five Cent Savings Bank	"
Cambridgeport National Bank	Cambridgeport.
National City Bank	Lynn.
American National Bank	Hartford, Conn.
Mercantile National Bank	" "
Birmingham " "	Birmingham, "
Central " "	Middletown, "
Waterbury " "	Waterbury, "
Middlesex County National Bank	Middletown, "
Employees of above Bank	" "
New Haven County National Bank	New Haven, "
First National Bank	Augusta, Maine.
Granite National Bank	" "
First National Bank	Concord, "
Calais " "	Calais, "
Freemans " "	Augusta, "
Kennebec Savings Bank	" "

110 *ROBBER AND HERO.*

Cabbassee National Bank	Gardiner, Maine.
Gardiner National Bank	" "
Bath National Bank	Bath, Maine.
Falls Village Savings Bank	" "
Third National Bank	Providence, R. I.
Bank of North America	" "
Slater National Bank	Pawtucket, "
Rhode Island National Bank	Weybasset, "
Rockingham National Bank	Portsmouth, N. H.
Strafford National Bank	Dover, "
National State Capital Bank	Concord, "
Bank of Derby Line	Derby, Vt.
Montpelier National Bank	Montpelier, "
Niantic National Bank	Westerly, R. I.

NEW YORK.

National Bank	West Troy.
Bank of America	New York.
Tanners National Bank	Catskill.
J. G. Munro	Buffalo.
Marine Bank	"
H. F. Spaulding, Pres. Central Trust Co.	New York.
Brown Bros. & Co.	" "
Importers & Traders Natl. Bank	" "
Farmers & Mechanics Natl. Bank	Buffalo.
F. R. Delano & Co.	Niagara Falls.
Ten Banks in	Syracuse.
Lyons National Bank	Lyons.
Manufacturers National Bank	Troy.
First National Bank	New York.
Fisk & Hatch	" "
E. P. Cook	Havane.
National Central Bank	Cherry Valley.
National Bank of Salem	Salem.
Merchants National Bank	New York.
Munroe County Savings Bank	Rochester.
Mechanics National Bank	New York.
G. H. Smith	Haverstraw.

City Bank	Oswego.
Manufacturers National Bank	Williamsburg.
Bank of North America	New York.
Manhattan Co.	" "
Metropolitan National Bank	" "
W. W. Astor	" "
Gallatin Natl. Bank	" "
Executive Commercial Mercantile Trust Co.	" "
First National Bank	Red Hook.
" " "	Jamestown.
Farmers National Bank	Amsterdam.
Chemical " "	New York.
New York Savings Bank	" "
American Exch. National Bank	" "
J. T. Foote	" "
First National Bank	Champlain.
Witmer Bros.	Suspension Bridge.
City National Bank	Jamestown.
Manufacturers Bank	Cohoes.
C. P. Williams	Albany.
First National Bank	Rondout.
Third " "	New York.

MISSOURI.

Bank of Holden	Holden.
People's Savings Bank	Chillicothe.
Third National "	St. Louis.
Montgomery County Bank	Montgomery City.
Boone Co. National "	Columbia.
First " "	St. Joseph.
Bank of Joplin	Joplin.
First National Bank	Kansas City.
Scotland County Bank	Memphis.
Farmers & Drovers Bank	Carthage.
Bank of Commerce	St. Louis.
First National Bank	Paris.
Lawrence County Bank	Pierce City.
Franklin Abe. Germ. Sav. Institution	St. Louis.

Waverly Bank   Waverly.
Aull Savings Bank   Lexington.

TENNESSEE.

First National Bank   Chattanooga.
Commercial National Bank   Knoxville.

OHIO.

Jos. F. Larkin & Co.   Cincinnati.
Ramsey & Teeple   Delta.
Farmers Bank   Wapakoneta.
Second National Bank   Toledo.
First   "   "   Massillon.
First   "   "   Portsmouth.
Harrison National Bank   Cadiz.
Commercial National Bank   Cleveland.
Barber & Merrill   Wauseon.
First National Bank   Troy.
Merchants National Bank   Dayton.
Youngstown Sav. & Loan Association   Youngstown.
Wicks Bros. & Co.   "
Second National Bank   "
First   "   "   "
   "   "   "   Springfield.
   "   "   "   East Liverpool.
   "   "   "   Ashland.

MICHIGAN.

Second National Bank   Detroit.
   "   "   "   Hillsdale.
First   "   "   Plymouth.
   "   "   "   St. Joseph.
   "   "   "   Port Huron.
Randall & Darrah   Grand Rapids.
National Bank of Michigan   Marshall.
Boies, Rude & Co.   Hudson.
First National Bank   Houghton.
   "   "   "   Dowagiac.
Ann Arbor Savings Bank   Ann Arbor.

Perkins, Thompson & Co.	Hudson.
First National Bank	Hancock.
Merchants & Miners Bank	Calumet.

INDIANA.

Richmond National Bank	Richmond.
Fort Wayne " "	Fort Wayne.
Citizens " "	Jeffersonville.
First " "	New Albany.
Brazil Bank	Brazil.
Walkers Bank	Kokoma.
Citizens National Bank	Greensburg.
National Branch Bank	Madison.
First National Bank	Richmond.
Citizens National Bank	Peru.
First National Bank	Tell City.

ILLINOIS.

First National Bank	Marseilles.
Commercial National Bank	Chicago.
Chicago Clearing House Association	Chicago.
Union National Bank	Aurora.
J. A. Beach	Bunker Hill.
"A Friend"	Girard.
Bank of Forreston	Forreston.
Geo. Wright	Paxton.
First National Bank	Peoria.
" " "	Princeton.
City " "	Cairo.
Peoples Bank	Bloomington.
Scott & Wrigley	Wyoming.
C. G. Cloud	McLeansboro.
Union National Bank	Streator.
Knowlton Bros.	Freeport.
Alton National Bank	Alton.
W. F. Thornton & Son	Shelbyville.
Farmers National Bank	Keithsburg.
First " "	Freeport.

First National Bank	Kankakee.
" " "	Ottawa.
Citizens " "	"
First " "	Quincy.
" " "	Arcola.
Edgar County National Bank	Paris.
Griggsville " "	Griggsville.
Cass County Bank	Beardstown.
First National "	Knoxville.
T. W. Raymond & Co.	Kinmundy.
Ridgely National Bank	Springfield.
First " "	Warsaw.
" " "	Shawneetown.
" " "	Rushville.
Stetson, Littlewood & Richards	Farmington.
First National Bank	Canton.
" " "	Centralia.

MAINE.

First National Bank	Brunswick.
West Waterville National Bank	West Waterville.
First National Bank	Damariscotta.
People's National Bank	Waterville.
Banks in	Portland.

VERMONT.

First National Bank	Fairhaven,
" " "	Orwell.

ARKANSAS.

National Bank Western Arkansas	Fort Smith.

CALIFORNIA.

Bank of Woodland	Woodland.
Caisse d'Epargnes Francaise	San Francisco.
Kern Valley Bank	Bakersfield.
First National Gold Bank	Oakland.
Nevada Bank	San Francisco.
Santa Barbara County Bank	Santa Barbara.

COLORADO.

First National Bank	Denver.
" " "	Trinidad.
Emerson & West	Greeley.
Colorado National Bank	Denver.

DAKOTA TERRITORY.

| Mark M. Parmer | Yankton. |

NEW HAMPSHIRE.

Claremont National Bank	Claremont.
Castleton " "	Castleton.
National Bank of Lebanon	Lebanon.
Littleton National Bank	Littleton.

TEXAS.

Ragnet & Fry	Marshall.
J R. Couts & Co	Weatherford.
Merchants & Planters Bank	Sherman.
First National Bank	Parsons.

RHODE ISLAND.

Roger Williams National Bank	Providence.
Manufacturers National Bank	"
Wasnington National Bank	Westerly.
National Phoenix Bank	"
National Exchange Bank	Providence.
Centreville National Bank	Centreville.
Warwick Institute for Savings	"
Merchants National Bank	Providence.

CONNECTICUT.

First National Bank	Middletown.
First National Bank	Stamford.
Phoenix National Bank	Hartford.
Geo. A. Butler	New Haven.
Banks of Bridgeport	Bridgeport.
Hartford National Bank	Hartford.
Deep River National Bank	Deep River.
Stamford National Bank	Stamford.

Farmers & Mechanics Sav. Bank	Middletown.
Norwich Savings Bank	Norwich.
Thames National Bank	Norwich.

PENNSYLVANIA.

First National Bank	Columbia.
First National Bank	Sharon.
Pittsburgh Clearing House Association	Pittsburgh.
National Bank	Pottstown.
First National Bank	Oil City.
National Bank, Chester Valley	Coatesville.
First National Bank	Pittston.
Watsontown Bank	Watsontown.
Cassatt & Co.	Philadelphia.
First National Bank	Shippensburg.
First National Bank Hanover	Hanover.
St. Petersburg Savings Bank	St. Petersburg
Marine National Bank	Erie.
National Bank, Fayette Co.	Uniontown.
National Bank, Chester Co.	Chester.
Marine National Bank	Pittsburgh.
Columbia National Bank	Columbia.
Citizens National Bank	Ashland.
Doylestown National Bank	Doylestown.
Spring Garden Bank	Philadelphia.
National Bank, Oxford	Oxford.
First National Bank	Altoona.
Commercial National Bank of Pennsylvania	Philadelphia.
National Bank Republic	"
Union National Bank	"
National Bank of	Phoenixville.
Farmers & Mechanics National Bank	"
Bank of North America	Philadelphia.
W. I. Du Bois	"
First National Bank	Strasburg.

IOWA.

| First National Bank | Bell Plaine. |
| Levitt, Johnson & Lursch | Waterloo. |

First National Bank	Boone.
First National Bank	Wyoming.
First National Bank	Decorah.
National State Bank	Burlington.
Conger, Pierce & Co.	Dexter.
E. Manning	Keosaugua.
First National Bank	Chariton.
Citizens National Bank	Winterset.
H. F. Greef & Bro.	Beautonsport.
Council Bluffs Savings Bank	Council Bluffs.
Greene County Bank	Jefferson.
Muscatine National Bank	Muscatine.
State National Bank	Keokuk.
First National Bank	Red Oak.
Davenport National Bank	Davenport.
Bank of Carroll	Carroll City.
Cerro Gordo County Bank	Mason City.
Clinton National Bank	Clinton.
Silverman, Cook & Co.	Muscatine.
First National Bank	Grinnell.

KANSAS.

Topeka National Bank	Topeka.
Abilene Bank	Abilene.
Humboldt Bank	Humboldt.
D. W. Powers & Co.	Ellsworth.
Emporia National Bank	Emporia.
Turner & Otis	Independence.

MARYLAND.

First National Bank	Baltimore.
National Union Bank	Baltimore.
First National Bank	Westminster.
National Bank of Baltimore	Baltimore.

CANADA.

Merchants Bank, Canada	Hamilton.
Bank of Toronto	Toronto.
Thos. Fyshe	Halifax.

KENTUCKY.

Theo. Schwartz & Co.	Louisville.
National Bank of Cynthiana	Cynthiana.
German National Bank	Covington.

ALABAMA.

City National Bank	Selma.

SOUTH CAROLINA.

South Carolina Loan & Trust Co.	Charleston.
National Bank	Anderson.

MISSISSIPPI.

Vicksburg Bank	Vicksburg.

NEW JERSEY.

First National Bank	Morristown.

WISCONSIN.

First National Bank	Milwaukee.
National Exchange Bank	"
Manufacturers National Bank	Racine.
First National Bank	Whitewater.
Wisconsin Marine & Fire Ins. Co. Bank	Milwaukee.
First National Bank	Hudson.
Bank of Evansville	Evansville.
Batavian Bank	La Crosse.
National "	Delevan.
First National Bank	Monroe.
Bowman & Humbird	Black River Falls.
Milwaukee National Bank	Milwaukee.
German Bank	Sheboygan.
J. F. Cleghorn	Clinton.
Savings Bank	Fond du Lac.
Kellogg National Bank	Green Bay.
First " "	Madison.
Waukesha " "	Waukesha.
Marshall & Ilsley	Milwaukee.
Shullsburg Bank	Shullsburg.
First National Bank	Fond du Lac.

Humphry & Clark — Bloomington.
Second Ward Sav. Bank — Milwaukee.

DELAWARE.

Delaware City National Bank — Delaware City.
First National Bank — Wilmington.
Union " " — "
National Bank of Delaware — "
" " of Wilmington & B. W. — "
Newport National Bank — Newport.

WEST VIRGINIA.

Merchants National Bank of West Virginia. — Morganstown.
Commercial Bank — Wheeling.
Exchange " — "

VIRGINIA.

Planters & Mechanics Bank — Petersburg.
German Banking Co. — Alexandria.

LOUISIANA.

Citizens Bank of Louisiana — New Orleans.

GEORGIA.

Bank of Americus — Americus.

UTAH.

Deseret National Bank — Salt Lake City.

OREGON.

First National Bank — Portland.
Ladd & Tilton — "
One Unknown.

INDEX

Allen, J. S., merchant, 12; in raid, 14–15, 26–27, 30
Ames, J. T., organizes pursuit, 50
Anderson, Andrew, farmer, 67
Anderson, William ("Bloody Bill"), guerilla leader, xi

Barton, Ara, sheriff, 51, 75, 78
Baxter, G. N., prosecutor, 76
Billy the Kid, as hero, xv, xxvii, xxxii
Blue Earth River, fugitives cross, 58
Bradford, George A., pursues fugitives, 66, 69; wounded, 70; biographical note, 96–97
Bridge Square, Northfield, 9, 12, 15
Brissette, ——, detective, 52
Bronaugh, Warren Carter, leads campaign for pardons, xix(note)
Bunker, Alonzo E., bank teller, 17; in raid, 18–23; biographical note, 84–87
Bunker, Mrs. Alonzo E., 39, 85, 87

Cannon City, gang visits, 8
Cannon River, 8, 48
Carleton College, Northfield, ix, xiii, 9, 28, 39
Chadwell, William, see Stiles, William
Crittenden, Thomas T., governor, xiii, xix, xxi

Dampier, ——, clerk, 26, 33
Dampier Hotel, Northfield, 26
Davis, Cushman K., supports pardon, xxi
"Defeat of Jesse James Days," Northfield, xxx–xxxiii
Demming, Portius C., legislator, xxiii
Division Street, Northfield, 9, 12, 14, 15, 29
Donnelly, Ignatius, supports pardon, xxi
Dundas, fugitives visit, 48

Elysian Township, Le Sueur County, 55, 57
Estes, W. R., pursues fugitives, 65

121